Arthur W. Heilman

Professor Emeritus
The Pennsylvania State University

PHONICS IN PROPER PERSPECTIVE

Seventh Edition

Merrill, an imprint of
Macmillan Publishing Company
New York

Maxwell Macmillan Canada
Toronto

Maxwell Macmillan International
New York   Oxford   Singapore   Sydney

Cover Art: Tom Post
Editor: Linda James Scharp
Production Editor: Sheryl Glicker Langner
Art Coordinator: Peter A. Robison
Text Designer: Jill E. Bonar
Cover Designer: Cathleen Norz
Production Buyer: Pamela D. Bennett

This book was set in Frutiger Light by Carlisle Communications, Ltd. and was printed and bound by Book Press, Inc., a Quebecor America Book Group Company. The cover was printed by Phoenix Color Corp.

Macmillan Publishing Company
113 Sylvan Avenue, Englewood Cliffs, NJ 07632

Library of Congress Cataloging-in-Publication Data
  Heilman, Arthur W.
    Phonics in proper perspective / Arthur W. Heilman. -- 7th ed.
        p.   cm.
    Includes bibliographical references and index.
    ISBN 0-02-353065-0
    1. Reading (Elementary)--Phonetic method. I. Title.
  LB1573.3.H44 1993
  372.4' 145--dc20   92-12517
                                                                        CIP

Printing: 3 4 5 6 7 8 9   Year: 5 6 7

Preface

The purpose of this book is to provide both the experienced and the prospective teacher with materials that will lead to better understanding of:

- The purpose and limitations of phonics instruction as it relates to teaching reading
- Concrete practices to follow in teaching the various "steps" in phonics analysis
- The rationale that underlies particular instructional practices

The material in this book reflects several premises:

- Phonics is an important part of teaching beginning reading.
- Teachers should be knowledgeable about the purpose of phonics instruction and its limitations.
- For children to make normal progress in learning to read, they must learn to associate printed letter forms with the speech sounds they represent.
- Beginning reading instruction must not mislead children into thinking that reading is sounding out letters, learning sight words, or using context clues.

Learning to read involves *all* these skills in the right combination. The optimum amount of phonics instruction for each child is the absolute minimum the child needs to become an independent reader. Excessive phonics instruction will usurp time that should be devoted to reading, can destroy children's interest in reading, and may lead critics to attack phonics instruction rather than bad phonics instruction.

Some teaching exercises in Chapters 5, 6, and 7 incorporate phonics instruction with reading for meaning. These materials illustrate the point that all phonics instruction need not be viewed as an additive which is unrelated to language and context.

For the seventh edition, I would like to thank the following reviewers who provided valuable comments and suggestions: William S. O'Bruba, Bloomsburg University; Nancy B. Keller, State University of New York at Oneonta; Kay G. Rayborn, Stephen F. Austin State University; and Dorothy A. Wedge, Fairmont State College.

Contents

Chapter 1   Phonics: Purpose and Limitations   1

The Study of Phonics   1
Variability of Letter Sounds in English   5

Chapter 2   Phonics: History and Controversy   9

Early Crimes Against Children   9
Sight-Word Method vs. Phonetic Method   11
Criticism Leads to New Materials   12
The Initial Teaching Alphabet (i.t.a.)   12
The Linguistic (Regular Spelling) Approach   16
Programmed Reading   21
Words in Color   22

Chapter 3   Phonics and Reading Instruction   25

How Children Learn to Read   26
Overview of Word Analysis Skills   28
Skills in Combination   30
Instructional Issues in Phonics Instruction   32
Principles to Apply in Teaching Phonics   35

Chapter 4   Prerequisites for Phonics Instruction   37

Visual Discrimination   37
Auditory Discrimination   43

Chapter 5   Teaching Consonant Letter-Sound Relationships   51

A Word about Sequence   51
Consonants in Initial Position   52
Context Clues and Phonic Skills: Working Together   59
Teaching Consonant Blends   63
Teaching Consonant Digraphs (*sh*, *wh*, *th*, *ch*)   68
Consonant Sounds at Ends of Words   73
Consonant Irregularities   77

Chapter 6   Teaching Vowel Letter-Sound Relationships   85

Phonics Instruction as Overkill   85
Sequence in Teaching Vowel Letter-Sounds   86
Teaching Short Vowel Sounds   87
The Long Vowel (Glided) Letter Sounds   95
Exceptions to Vowel Rules Previously Taught   102
Vowel Sounds Affected by *R*   103

A Followed by *L*, *LL*, *W*, and *U*   104

The *oo* Sounds   104

Diphthongs   105

Homonyms   107

The Schwa Sound   110

Sight-Word List   110

Chapter 7   Structural Analysis Skills   113

Inflectional Endings   114

Words Ending with *e*   115

Doubling Final Consonants   116

Compound Words   118

Working with Plurals   122

Prefixes and Suffixes   126

Syllabication   129

Abbreviations   133

Recognizing Contractions   134

Finding Little Words in Big Words   136

Accent   136

Stress on Words within Sentences   138

Use of the Dictionary—As a Word Attack Skill   138

References   141

Index   143

1

Phonics: Purpose and Limitations

The purpose of phonics instruction is to teach beginning readers that printed letters and letter-combinations represent speech sounds heard in words. In applying phonic skills to an unknown word, the reader blends a series of sounds dictated by the order in which particular letters occur in the printed word. One needs this ability to arrive at the pronunciation of printed word symbols that are not instantly recognized. Obviously, if one recognizes a printed word, he should not puzzle over the speech sounds represented by the individual letters.

"Arriving at the pronunciation" of a word does not mean learning *how* to pronounce that word. In most reading situations, particularly in the primary grades, the reader knows the pronunciation of practically all words he will meet in his reading. What he does not know is that the printed word symbol *represents* the pronunciation of a particular word he uses and understands in oral language. Through phonic analysis he resolves this dilemma. Phonic analysis is an absolutely essential skill in beginning reading.

The Study of Phonics

Phonics is not a *method* of teaching reading, nor is it the same as phonetics. Phonics is one of a number of ways a child may "solve" words not known as sight words.

Phonics instruction is concerned with teaching letter-sound relationships *only as they relate to learning to read.* English spelling patterns being what they are, a child will sometimes arrive at only a close approximation of the needed sounds. He may pronounce *broad* so it rhymes with *road,* or *fath* (in father) so that it rhymes with *path.* Fortunately, if he is reading for meaning, he will instantly correct these errors. After a few such self-corrections, he will never again make these particular mistakes.

Phonetics is much more precise. It is the scientific study of the sound systems of language. A phonetician is a scientist. He knows much more about speech sounds and spelling patterns than is necessary for the child to know while learning to read, or for the teacher to teach when the goal is teaching reading.

Linguists rightfully urge reading teachers not to confuse phonics with phonetics. Phonetics is a science; the teaching of reading is not. While it is true that phonics is based on phonetics, linguists should not be distressed when they observe a phonics instruction program that does not include certain known phonetic data. First and second graders do not need to be exposed to all the phonetic data that have been assembled. Learning to read is a complicated process, and it need not be complicated further simply because a vast body of phonetic data exists. In teaching reading, one must hold to the scientific principle that instruction follow the most economical path to its chosen goal. A guideline for instruction is that *the optimum amount of phonics instruction a child should be exposed to is the minimum the child needs to become an independent reader.* This is certainly not the way to become a linguist, but it is good pedagogy for beginning reading instruction.

Terminology

In recent years, noticeable confusion has accompanied discussions of reading because the meaning of some of the terms used was vague or misleading. To eliminate further confusion, we will briefly define a few basic terms.

Alphabetic principle.   Graphic symbols have been devised for representing a large number of spoken languages. Three types of writing (picture, ideographic, and alphabetic) represent the English words or concepts *car, carp,* and *carpet* (Figure 1–1).

The picture and ideographic writing are purely arbitrary. The ideographs are not taken from an established language. The most important feature of the ideographic writing is that there are no common features in the three symbols. The alphabetic writing is also arbitrary, but the letter symbols and their order of occurrence have been universally agreed upon since they are taken from English writing. The first three letter-symbols in each word are identical. They signal the reader to blend the same three speech sounds (phonemes) if the goal is to arrive at the spoken word that the various letter configurations represent. In the case of *carp* and *carpet,* the reader must blend still other phonemes.

There are many other spoken words in which one hears the same three phonemes in the same sequence. The graphic representation of these speech sounds will be the same in a number of printed words: *carnival, cardinal, card, cartoon.* In English writing, however, one may see the graphic symbols *car* and find they represent different phonemes from the ones under discussion (*carol, care, career, caress, caret*).

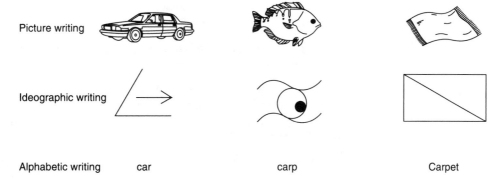

Figure 1–1 appears with labels:
Picture writing
Ideographic writing
Alphabetic writing   car   carp   Carpet

Figure 1–1 Three types of writing

Cracking the code.   This term is generally used to describe the process of learning to associate printed letters with the speech sounds they represent. In a discussion of beginning reading, cracking the code refers to learning letter-sound relationships via the ability to apply phonics. When a child has learned to associate all of the specific printed letters with specific speech sounds, the code has been mastered, or cracked. The child now can arrive at or approximate the pronunciation of most printed word symbols.

Digraph.   Combinations of two letters that represent one speech sound (consonant examples: *church, show, thank*; vowels: b*ee*t, c*oa*t, m*ai*l).

Diphthong.   A vowel blend; two adjacent vowels each of which is sounded (ou in h*ou*se; oi in *oi*l; oy in b*oy;* ow in h*ow*).

Grapheme.   A written or printed letter-symbol used to represent a speech sound or phoneme.

Grapheme-phoneme relationship.   This term refers to the relationship between printed letters and the sounds they represent; it would also cover the deviations found in such a relationship. Thus, while English writing is based on an alphabetic code, there is not a one-to-one relationship between graphemes (printed symbols) and the phonemes (speech sounds) they represent. Some printed symbols represent several different sounds (car, caress, cake), and one speech sound may be represented by a large number of different letters or combination of letters (which we will discuss later in this chapter). To a large extent, this problem stems from the spelling patterns of words that have become established in English writing.

Morphemes.   The smallest meaningful units of language. The word *cat* is a morpheme whose pronunciation consists of three phonemes. If one wishes to speak of more than one cat, the letter *s* forming the plural cat*s* becomes a morpheme, since it changes the meaning (as does the possessive *'s* in the *cat's dinner*).

There are two classes of morphemes, free and bound. The former functions independently in any utterance (*house, lock, man, want*). Bound morphemes consist of prefixes, suffixes, and inflectional endings and must combine with other mor-phemes (house*s*, *un*lock, man*'s*, want*ed*).

Phoneme. The smallest unit of sound in a language that distinguishes one word from another. Pronouncing the word *cat* involves blending three phonemes: /k/ /æ/ /t/ .

Phonetic method. The term "phonetic method" is a vague term that was used to indicate instruction that included phonics, emphasized phonics, or overemphasized phonics. Eventually it acquired the "polar connotation" pro-phonics and anti-sight-word method. (We will discuss this dichotomy in chapter 2.)

Phonetics. That segment of linguistic science that deals with (a) speech sounds; (b) how these sounds are made vocally; (c) sound changes that develop in languages; and (d) the relation of speech sounds to the total language process. All phonics instruction is derived from phonetics, but phonics as it relates to reading utilizes only a relatively small portion of the body of knowledge identified as phonetics.

Phonic analysis. The process of applying knowledge of letter-sound relationships, that is, blending the sounds represented by letters so as to arrive at the pronunciation of printed words.

Phonics instruction. A facet of reading instruction that (a) leads the child to un-derstand that printed letters in printed words represent the speech sounds heard when words are pronounced; and (b) involves the actual teaching of which sound is associated with a particular letter or combination of letters.

Schwa. The schwa sound is a diminished stress, or a softening of the vowel sound. Schwa is represented by the symbol ə (bedlam = bed ləm; beckon = bek'ən). Any of the vowels may represent the schwa sound.

Sight vocabulary. Any words a reader recognizes instantly, without having to resort to any word recognition strategies.

Sight-word method. The term "sight-word method" is an abstraction rather than a description of reading instruction. Some beginning reading materials devel-oped in the first half of the century, however, advocated teaching a limited number of sight words before phonic analysis was introduced. The term sight-word method became common even though it actually described only this initial teaching proce-dure. Gradually the term was used to imply the existence of an instructional approach that allegedly proscribed phonics and advocated teaching every new word by sight only.

Word analysis. An inclusive term that refers to all methods of word recognition. Phonics is one such method.

Limitations of Phonics

Phonics instruction does have limitations. Knowing this fact helps us avoid expecting too much of our lessons. It also helps us see why children need other related word recognition skills.

Variability of Letter Sounds in English

The greatest limitation on the use of phonics is the spelling patterns of many English words. Although written English is alphabetic, the irregular spellings of words prevent anything like a one-to-one relationship between letters seen and sounds heard. Some of the reasons for, and examples of, this problem are

1. Many English words have come from other languages such as Latin, Greek, French, and German (*waive, alias, corps, debris, alien, buoy, feint, bouquet*). The spelling of these words is often confusing.
2. A given letter, or letters, may represent different sounds in different words: (*cow* = [ow], *low* = [ō]; *can* = [ă;], *cane* = [ā]; *cap* = [k], *city* = [s]; *bus* = [s], *his* = [z], *measure* = [zh]).

The following illustrate some of the variability found in English words. Some words (homonyms) are (a) pronounced the same, (b) spelled differently, and (c) each is phonetically "lawful":

weak — week	meat — meet	heal — heel	beat — beet
sail — sale	maid — made	pain — pane	mail — male

In these examples, the generalization that applies to both spellings is *when there are two vowels in a word, usually the first is long and the second is not sounded.*

One word in each of the following pairs is governed by this phonic generalization; the other is not.

ate	rain	peace	wait
eight	reign	piece	weight

In hundreds of English words a letter or letters may represent no sound:

nig*h*t	com*b*	of*t*en	*w*rong

A word may have one or more letters (not sounded) that differentiate it from another word pronounced exactly the same:

new	our	plum	cent	no
knew	hour	plumb	scent	know

The long sound of vowels may be represented by any of these and other combinations in words:

	day	they	fate	sail	reign	great
ā =	*ay*	*ey*	*a*(e)	*ai*	*ei*	*ea*
	feet	meat	deceive	brief	ski	key
ē =	*ee*	*ea*	*ei*	*ie*	*i*	*ey*
	my	kite	pie	height	buy	guide
ī =	*y*	*i*(e)	*ie*	*ei*	*uy*	*ui*

	show	hold	boat	note	go	sew
ō =	ow	o (+ ld)	oa	o(e)	o	ew
	flew	view	tube	due	suit	you
ū =	ew	iew	u	ue	ui	ou

One of the problems in teaching letter-sound relationships, is that dozens of "rules" or "generalizations" have been developed to help learners arrive at the pronunciation of words they do not recognize. The following discussion focuses on three of the most widely used generalizations and their limited efficacy due to numerous exceptions.

1. *Two vowels together, the first is long and the second is not sounded.*
   applies: boat, rain, meat, week, soap, sail, need.
   exceptions: been, said, chief, dead, field, head, their.
2. *In two-vowel words, the final e is silent and the previous vowel usually has its long sound.*
   applies: ride, pale, hate, bite, dime, hide, cane, cute.
   exceptions: love, done, have, come, give, none, once.
   Extensive research has shown that the above rules apply less than fifty percent of the time in high frequency words.
3. *A single vowel in medial position in a word or syllable usually has its short sound.*

This generalization can be useful to children learning to read. It applies to enough high frequency words to justify calling it to the students' attention. However, there is no phonetic rule that will apply to all words that meet the criteria the rule sets forth. The following illustrates how, when a rule does not apply to a number of words, a new rule emerges to cover this situation.

There are also a number of consonant irregularities (discussed in chapter 5), but none of these represent the large number of sounding options that are characteristic of vowels.

Exception A: *hold, cold, bold, gold; bolt, colt.*
New rule: The single vowel *o*, followed by *ld* or *lt,* has its long sound.

Exception B: *car, fir, fur, her, for, part, bird, hurt, perch, corn.*
New rule: A vowel followed by *r* has neither its long nor short sound—the vowel sound is modified by the *r.*

Exception C: *wild, mild, child; find, kind, mind, blind.*
New rule: The vowel *i* before *ld* or *nd* is usually long.

Exception D: *fall, call, ball; salt, malt, halt.*
New rule: The vowel *a* followed by *ll* or *lt* is pronounced like *aw* (ball = bawl).

Exception E: *high, sigh; light, night, bright, flight.*
New rule: The vowel *i* in *igh* or *ight* words is usually long.

Other exceptions: *sign* = (i); *was* = (u); *both* = (ō); *front* = (u).

These examples deal only with monosyllabic words containing a single vowel in a medial position. The "exceptions" to the basic rule are only the major ones that might logically be dealt with in teaching reading, and the words listed represent only a small fraction of those that could be cited. As rules become more involved and cover fewer and fewer actual words, one may question the relationship between learning these rules and learning the process called reading.

In recent years, teachers have had considerable data available that focus on the frequency with which various phonic rules apply to words children will meet in their primary and elementary school experiences. Studies by Oaks, Clymer, Bailey, Emans, Burmeister, and Burrows and Lourie are in agreement in their findings that there are a significant number of exceptions to generalizations covering vowel sounds.

The educational issue is not arriving at a universally agreed upon list of rules to be taught. The real problem, which is much more complicated, is what happens to learners under various types of instruction that focus on rules. What types of attack strategies do children develop? There is little information to guide teachers. Those who have worked extensively with impaired readers have undoubtedly encountered some children who are "rule-oriented." Some of these children persist in trying to make the rule fit even when the word they are attacking is an exception. Others can cite the rule and are still unable to apply it to words that it covers.

Despite the absence of data that might serve as a guide for teaching phonic generalizations, teachers must decide on the teaching strategies they will use. They may choose instructional materials that make a fetish of memorizing phonic generalizations. They might, on the other hand, present a series of words governed by a particular rule and invite children to formulate a generalization. The latter course seems preferable, not just because it fits under the rubric *discovery method,* but because it permits children to work with concepts they can understand. Furthermore, it relieves the learning situation of a certain degree of rigidity and reduces the finality that is usually associated with a rule.

2

Phonics: History and Controversy

Today, American public education is under siege. The issue, spoken or not, is how can we gracefully repeal the American dream of universal free education, which results in educating every child to the maximum of his ability? Neither educators nor their critics believe the schools can educate all of the children that our society delivers to the schools. A few decades ago criticism of American education focused almost entirely on reading, or more precisely, on the phonics component of that instruction.

Should educators, and specifically reading teachers, be conversant with past instructional methods and materials? It might be difficult to establish that knowledge of this history is essential for successful teaching of reading. However, such knowledge can be helpful in understanding some of the problems, attitudes, and misunderstandings which have been and still are associated with American reading instruction.

Early Crimes Against Children

During the latter part of the nineteenth century, beginning reading instruction stressed the teaching of the ABC's. Children were taught to recite the names of the letters which made up unknown words met in reading. It was believed that letter naming would provide the necessary phonetic clues for arriving at the spoken word the printed symbols represented. In essence, this was a spelling approach, since letter "names" often had little resemblance to speech sounds represented by letters (*come = see oh em ee = kum*). This approach, abandoned because it didn't work, was revived in 1961 by Bloomfield.

Prior to 1900, and continuing for over a decade, emphasis shifted from drill on letter "names" to drill on the "sounds of the various letters." Rebecca Pollard's *Synthetic Method,* introduced about 1890, advocated reducing reading to a number of mechanical procedures, each of which focused on a unit smaller than a word. Reading became very mechanistic and, when mastered, often produced individuals who were adept at working their way through a given word. The result among both teachers and pupils was that reading became equated with "facility in calling words." A few of the recommended procedures of this method were:

1. Drills in articulation were to precede any attempt at reading. The child was to drill on the "sounds of letters." Then the child would be able, it was reasoned, to attack whole words.
2. Single consonants were "sounded." Each consonant was given a sound equivalent to a syllable. Thus *b, c, d, p, h,* and *t* were sounded *buh, cuh, duh, puh, huh,* and *tuh.*
3. Drills on word families were stressed, without regard for word meanings. Sometimes children memorized lists of words ending in such common family phonograms as *ill, am, ick, ate, old, ack.*
4. Diacritical markings were introduced in first grade, and children drilled on "marking sentences." For example: The ghŏst wăs ā cŏmmŏn sīght near the wrĕck. He knew the īsland was ĕmpty.

This and similar approaches had a number of weaknesses including:

1. The sounds assigned to consonant letters were arbitrary.
2. Letter sounds were overemphasized and taught in isolation (*buh-ah-tuh = bat*).
3. This was true also as drill on vowel letter-sounds was combined with initial consonant sounds (*ba, da, ha, ma, pa, ra,* etc.).
4. Drill instruction was not related to actual words or to "reading."

It is easy to see that this type of instruction placed little emphasis on reading as a "meaning making" process. As children performed these ritualistic drills, they developed an inappropriate concept of reading which influenced their reading behavior.

Dissatisfaction with this type of reading instruction led to criticism which focused on "too much emphasis on the sounds of the letters." The obvious reaction occurred—the instructional pendulum swung in the opposite direction. However, instead of modifying or reforming the offending instructional practices, the whole area of phonics fell under suspicion and attack. Apparently, this formula for solving instructional problems generated considerable appeal. Henceforth, whenever frustration with a pupil's reading ability reached a certain threshold, phonics instruction—or its alleged absence—was blamed for the problem. Just as the path of a pendulum can be predicted, so also can criticism and "reform" of reading instruction. Reform always involved advocating one of two polar positions:

1. the need for *more* phonics instruction;
2. the need for *less* phonics instruction.

Unfortunately, this oversimplification set the stage for decades of fruitless debate within the reading establishment. While the terms *more* or *less* phonics provided enough polarity, they were too mundane to lure proponents into devoting their lives to the cause. The problem was solved with the emergence of the linguistic mix of sight words vs. phonics, which came about as follows.

Sight-Word Method vs. Phonetic Method

Although phonics was out of favor during the 1930s and 1940s, some letter-sound relationships continued to be taught. This instruction was now less overt and less systematic. Gradually the conventional wisdom decreed that children should learn a number of sight words prior to receiving any phonics instruction. This philosophy, then reflected in many of the materials that were used in the schools, had a tendency to delay phonics instruction. Somehow this instructional philosophy became labeled the "sight-word method."

It is probably safe to surmise that the term "sight-word method" led some people to believe that there was such a method. Since the term omits any reference to phonics, some people might have inferred that phonics was meant to be excluded. At the other end of the continuum, the same type of illogical labeling was taking place. A belief that letter-sound relationships should be taught made one an advocate of the "phonetic method." Gradually, these two terms took on an either-or connotation and these were the only positions available. One was either pro-phonics and opposed to teaching sight words—or vice versa.

Although these labels could not, and did not, describe any instructional programs in the school, they completely dominated the debate on reading instruction. Hundreds of research articles, most of them of dubious quality, divided quite evenly on espousing either the phonetic or sight-word method. Thus, the twenty-year period preceding the 1950s did not witness any significant modifications in either instructional materials or methodology. All of the widely used basal reading programs were quite similar.

This period was characterized by indecision and confusion with reference to the role of phonics in teaching reading. The confusion then became apparent in the classroom behaviors of teachers. The frustration and criticisms which followed culminated in the inevitable demands for reforms of reading instruction.

Two quite different instructional thrusts emerged. One of these was the "individualized reading movement" which attacked basal reader materials, particularly workbooks. Pupil self-selection of reading materials and self-pacing in learning to read were advocated. In essence, individualized reading was a revolt against structured instructional materials and the "teaching of *isolated skills*." This latter term eventually became a code word for phonics instruction which was presented via workbooks.

In 1956, Rudolph Flesch's book *Why Johnny Can't Read* was the counterthrust to individualized reading. Both chose the same enemies—the established methods and materials used in reading instruction. However, Flesch's book was one-dimensional in that lack of phonics instruction was the alleged problem, and more phonics was the only acceptable solution. There was, he claimed, a conspiracy within the reading establishment to prevent the teaching of phonics. Institutions involved with teacher preparation were a part of, and a moving force behind, this conspiracy. Having identified the problem, he advanced a solution: teach phonics my way and there will be no failures in learning to read. This publication eventually triggered a strong swing of the pendulum back to phonics instruction.

Criticism Leads to New Materials

While Flesch was instrumental in arousing interest in phonics, his suggestions relative to teaching were quite primitive. His material consisted mostly of lists of words presenting different letter-sound patterns. Drill on these word lists was the extent of his instructional program. It was impossible for teachers to use these lists as a basis for instruction.

However, this instructional vacuum was soon filled with a number of new methods and materials which were developed and vigorously promoted. Many of these were designed primarily to supplement other programs such as existing basal reading series. In addition to the supplementary phonics materials, several "new approaches" to teaching reading appeared.

Schools were so willing to believe the promises of salvation offered by each new material that the 1960s were characterized as "the decade of the frantic search for a panacea" (Heilman, 1977). The purpose of the following discussion is to very briefly explain the rationale and the instructional program of a number of teaching materials which emerged at this time. Each of these had several common characteristics which merit close attention:

1. The major thrust of each method/material was to "crack the code" or the relationship between letters seen and the speech sounds these letters represented. (Note: All of these materials, except one, stressed systematic, hard-nosed teaching of phonics. The remaining approach attacked and proscribed phonics teaching.)
2. Each method depended on a new set of materials which was required for teaching that method.
3. Each approach focused *only* on beginning reading instruction. None provided an instructional program beyond the beginning stages.

The Initial Teaching Alphabet (i.t.a.)

The *Initial Teaching Alphabet* was developed in England by Sir James Pitman in order to achieve a more uniform "letter-seen sound-heard" relationship in English writing. These materials were first called the *Augmented Roman Alphabet,* since it consisted of 44 rather than 26 letter symbols (Figure 2–1).

The use of 44 symbols permits a much closer approximation of a one-to-one relationship between printed letters and the sounds they represent. Obviously, teach-

FIGURE 2–1 Pitman's Initial Teaching Alphabet (i.t.a.)

From Richard Fink and Patricia Keiserman, *i.t.a. Teacher Training Workbook and Guide* (New York: Initial Teaching Alphabet Publications, 1969). Reprinted by permission.

ing with i.t.a. involved the use of reading materials printed in i.t.a. Since the materials are concerned only with initial instruction, learners had to transfer from i.t.a. materials to materials printed in regular orthography, sometime near the end of first grade.

The Instructional Program

i.t.a. involves more than just the use of a modified orthography. There are several salient instructional features that are an integral part of its methodology.

1. Children were not taught letter names, but they were taught that each i.t.a. symbol represented a particular sound. Early instruction consisted of systematic teaching of these symbol-sound relationships.
2. From the very beginning of instruction, children were taught to write using the i.t.a. symbols. Writing, which involves spelling of words, reinforced the phonics instruction (letter-sound relationships).

3. In i.t.a. instruction, children learn only the lowercase letters. Capitals are indicated simply by making the letter larger. Thus the child does not have to deal with two different symbols for the same letter (A a, B b, C c, D d, E e, F f, G g, H h) in the initial stages of learning to read and write. In essence, what this practice does is to *delay* for a time the child's need to master both sets of symbols. That the child must deal with both capital and lowercase letters when transferring from i.t.a. to traditional print is one possible cause for the discrepancy between hoped for and actual ease in transferring (discussed later in the chapter).

4. Promotional materials for i.t.a. claimed that there was a high degree of compatibility between i.t.a. and traditional spellings and that this would facilitate the child's transfer from i.t.a. to regular print. In addition to the differences in typography, another fact often overlooked is that i.t.a. materials frequently resorted to phonetic respelling of irregularly spelled words.

i.t.a. – Medium or Method

Obviously, the *Initial Teaching Alphabet* taken by itself is not a method of teaching reading. When i.t.a. was first introduced in the United States, its proponents stressed that it was exclusively a medium and not a method. In an article, "Common Misconceptions about i.t.a.," Downing (1965) writes at considerable length on the issue. He states:

> To summarize this major point — i.t.a. is not a method of reading instruction and in particular, it is *not* to be associated with the synthetic phonics approach. On the contrary, i.t.a. is a system of printing for beginners books which may be used with any method — eclectic, phonics, look-say, language-experience, individualized, film strip, programmed learning, or any other. (p. 494)

The point of view that i.t.a. as a *medium* can be used equally effectively with any *method* ignores reality. The i.t.a. represents a redesigning of an existing alphabet for the express purpose of having printed letter symbols consistently represent one speech sound. There is no question but that the 44 character Initial Teaching Alphabet presents more of a problem in visual recognition than does the 26 character traditional alphabet. The potential virtue of the medium lies in the approximate one-to-one relationship between printed symbol and speech sound represented. Unless children learn this relationship and use it, there would be little point in advocating the revised alphabet.

Yet the designers of i.t.a., in order to evade being identified with one or the other side in the "sight-word vs. phonics method" controversy, maintain that i.t.a. can be used with either approach. Assume a reading method existed which relied on teaching whole words. It would be most difficult to find any justification for using i.t.a. as a beginning medium for teaching whole words if one is to transfer to traditional print after a year of instruction. What could possibly transfer? How would a child know that *wunz* was the same word as *once,* or that *waukt* equalled *walked?*

Methodological Practices Involved in i.t.a.

The mere choice of instructional materials printed in i.t.a. represents an important methodological decision. This decision, if based on logic, would then be followed by methodological considerations which grow out of the original choice. The i.t.a. involves more than just the use of a modified orthography. There are several salient instructional features which were an integral part of i.t.a. methodology used in American schools. A discussion of these follows.

i.t.a. — Postponing the Difficult

As the titles *Initial Teaching Alphabet* and *Initial Teaching Medium* imply, this is an approach that focuses on beginning reading only. Beginning reading tasks are simplified in several ways.

1. Capital letter forms are not introduced.
2. Irregularly spelled words are respelled.
3. All long vowel sounds are represented by two adjacent vowel letters.

Particular attention should be paid to the various respellings which result in a high degree of consistency between letters seen and sounds heard. This would have great virtue if it represented a real spelling reform. However, at time of transfer, children have to face the reality of irregular spellings while having been taught that words can be sounded by blending the sounds of the letters seen. This "reader set" developed during initial teaching can easily inhibit growth when irregular spellings are met in great profusion in traditional orthography. Table 2–1 illustrates respellings which have nothing to do with the modified alphabet.

Some of these respellings change the visual pattern of words quite drastically, which will not facilitate transfer to traditional print and spelling. While this practice might result in a fast start in beginning reading, it will have minimal effects on children cracking the main code. They must eventually deal with irregular words when they transfer to traditional orthography.

In addition to the phonetic respellings which do not involve any of the new i.t.a. characters, many spelling changes involve a reshuffling of vowels. The vowel changes and transpositions are made so that the spelling will follow the "two-vowel generalization" (when two vowels come together, the first has its long sound and the second is silent). A few examples follow in Table 2–2.

TABLE 2–1

enough - - - - - enuf	anyone - - - enywun	said - - - - - sed
come - - - - - - cum	once - - - - wuns	large - - - - larj
next - - - - - - - nekst	lovely - - - luvly	many - - - meny
George - - - - - Jorj	more - - - - mor	crossed - - - crosst
have - - - - - - - hav	some - - - - sum	one - - - - - wun
six - - - - - - - - siks	mother - - - muther	money - - - muny
couple - - - - - cupl	glove - - - - gluv	half - - - - - haf
laugh - - - - - - laf	none - - - - - nun	squirt - - - - skwirt
wax - - - - - - - waks	ought - - - - aut	someone - - sumwun
yacht - - - - - - yot	tough - - - -tuf	trouble - - - trubl

TABLE 2–2

also - - - - - - auls œ	night - - - - niet	find - - - - - f iend
their - - - - - thær	so - - - - - - - s œ	seized - - - - s ee zd
there - - - - - - thær	idea - - - - - ie d ee a	wife - - - - - w ie f
I - - - - - - - - ie	most - - - - mœst	walked - - - w au kt
knows - - - - - n œs	came - - - - c æm	ate - - - - - - æt
fire - - - - - - fie r	lace - - - - - l æ s	owe - - - - - œ
my - - - - - - - m ie	phone - - - f œ n	page - - - - pæj
sight - - - - - sie t	weigh - - - - w æ	gave - - - - - g æ v
giant - - - - - j ie ant	nice - - - - - n ie s	people - - - p ee pl
eyes - - - - - - ie s	five - - - - - f ie v	life - - - - - l ie f

Transfer from i.t.a. to Traditional Orthography

Concurrently with the introduction and use of i.t.a. in America, there were assurances from many quarters that *transfer* from i.t.a. to traditional print would not pose a problem. This optimism was allegedly grounded on reports from England. While Downing of England was actively promoting the experimental use of i.t.a. in America, his writing in 1963 on the issue of transfer contained a note of caution. He stated:

> If teachers *opinions* are supported by the results of the objective tests conducted last month (March 1963), we may feel encouraged in our *hopes* that all children will pass through the transfer stage with success, but *we must urge the greatest caution in drawing final conclusion or taking action on the basis of this preliminary trial.* . . . [Emphasis added] (p. 25)

In 1965, Downing was a bit more optimistic. "First results from our British i.t.a. research project seem to show that transfer is remarkably easy in reading and surprisingly effective in spelling" (p. 500). Downing's earlier caution was vindicated by the outcome of studies in England and America. In the December, 1967 issue of *Elementary English* Downing stated,

> Although teachers' subjective impressions of the transition stage have suggested that it is smooth and effortless, test results show that i.t.a. students from about mid-second year until about mid-third year do not read t.o. as well as they read i.t.a. a few weeks or even months previously. . . . More specifically, the British experiments show that children are not transferring from i.t.a. to t.o. in quite the way originally predicted. (p. 849)

Several studies in the U.S. reported data relative to students' ability to transfer to traditional orthography (Hayes & Nemeth, 1965; Mazurkiewicz, 1964). The success rates reported ranged from 26% to 74%. The criteria used to determine success was by necessity largely subjective.

The Linguistic (Regular Spelling) Approach

Of all the newer methods which emerged in the post-Flesch period, this one may well be the strangest. Attempting to deal with it briefly is difficult and frustrating. To many observers, it was a mystery how a noted and highly respected linguist like Leonard Bloomfield could espouse the system. A second mystery was why it was called a linguistic approach. Other than that the term "linguistic" was popular at the time, no explanation has emerged.

No branch of the science of linguistics has concerned itself with the problem of how children learn to read. Nevertheless, any linguist can address himself to this problem, and in recent years some linguists have done so. Their emphasis primarily has been on developing materials and methodology for *beginning reading instruction.*

The method/materials were first published in 1942. At that time they received little, if any, favorable response or acceptance. Yet, in the aftermath of *Why Johnny Can't Read* (which stressed phonics), the regular spelling material—which proscribed phonics—was resurrected and was able to pose successfully as a code-cracking approach, during one of the most pronounced "phonics emphasis" periods in history.

Premises of Linguistic Materials

Proscribing of pictures in beginning materials.   A minor premise, which is reflected in most of the teaching materials thus far prepared by linguists, is that pictures should be omitted from beginning reading materials. The assumption is that children might use the pictures for solving some unrecognized words and in so doing they would neglect the actual solving of the printed word symbols. This assumption, whether true or not, cannot be said to rest on any linguistic authority since there is nothing even remotely related to this issue in the science of linguistics.

Vocabulary control—(**regular spelling concept**).   Undoubtedly one of the major premises of linguists, who have thus far prepared reading instruction materials, is that *initial* instruction should be based exclusively on a unique vocabulary-control principle. This principle is that in early reading instruction the child should meet only those words which enjoy "regular spellings," a term used to designate words in which printed letters represent "the most characteristic sound" associated with each letter.

The word *cat* would meet this criterion, but the word *cent* would be *irregular* since the c does not represent the characteristic k sound but the sound usually represented by s. The spelling *bird* is irregular because the i represents a sound usually represented by u (burd) as does the o in *come* (kum).

In the regular spelling approach the child is first taught letter recognition and letter names (*aye, bee, see, dee, ee, eff*). Bloomfield suggests teaching both capital and small letters, while Fries advocates teaching capital letters only in initial instruction. After learning the letters in isolation, they are combined into words.

> The child need not even be told that the combinations are words; and he should certainly not be required to recognize or read words. *All he needs to do is read off the names of the successive letters, from left to right.* [Emphasis added] (Bloomfield, 1961, p. 36)

Then the child is ready to begin working his way through a series of words which end with identical letter-phoneme patterns (*can, fan, man, tan,* etc.). Bloomfield suggests that teaching should proceed as follows:

1. Print and point to the word CAN.
2. The child is to read the letters "see aye en."
3. The teacher states "now we have spelled the word. Now we are going to *read* it. This word is can. Read it *can*."
4. Present another word from the "an" family such as tan. (p. 41)

The aim of this teaching is to have the child distinguish between various words which differ only as to the initial grapheme-phoneme. However, the child is never DIRECTLY TAUGHT the association between the initial letter and the sound it represents in words. There is no question but that the child must learn this relationship in order to become an independent reader.

Unfortunately, a large number of the English words we use most frequently in building even the simplest of sentences have irregular spellings. Examples include: *a, the, was, once, of, any, could, love, too, their, do, said, one, who, some, only, gone, live, father, give, many, are, would, come, head, both, again, been, have, they, there, to, get, should,* etc. Normal English sentences are difficult to build when one decides to use only words which follow regular spelling patterns. For example, in Bloomfield's material, after 66 words have been taught (roughly equivalent to three preprimers in a representative basal series) one finds only the most contrived sentences and absolutely no story line:

> Pat had ham.
> Nat had jam.
> Sam had a cap.
> Dan had a hat.
> Sam ran.
> Can Sam tag Pam?
> Can Pam tag Sam? (p. 65)

After 200 words have been learned, the child reads these sentences:

> Let Dan bat. Did Al get wet? Van had a pet cat. Get up Tad! Let us in, Sis! Sis, let us in! Let Sid pet a pup. (p. 87)

Meaning waived in beginning instruction. Both Bloomfield and Fries, who developed materials based on regular spellings, reject the thesis that beginning reading instruction should be concerned with meaning. The rejection of meaning is not so much a well-founded pedagogical principle as it is an expediency when one is limited to using only those words which qualify as regular spellings.

Clarence Barnhart (1961), coauthor of *Let's Read,* states in the introduction:

> Bloomfield's system of teaching reading is a linguistic system. Essentially, a linguistic system of teaching reading separates the problem of the study of word-form from the study of word meaning. (p. 9)

Bloomfield wrote:

> Aside from their silliness, the stories in the child's first reader are of little use because the child is too busy with the mechanics of reading to get anything of the content. . . . This does not mean that we must forego the use of sentences and connected stories, but it does mean that these are not essential to the first steps. We need not fear to use disconnected words and even senseless syllables; and above all we must not, for

the sake of a story, upset the child's scarcely formed habits by presenting him with irregularities of spelling for which he is not prepared. (p. 34)

Fries (1963) was essentially in agreement when he wrote *Linguistics and Reading:*

Seeking an extraneous interest in a story as a story during the earliest steps of reading
is more likely to *hinder* than to help the efforts put forth by the reader himself.
(p. 199)

In a later writing Fries (1965) took the position:

. . . as a matter of fact the *primary objective* of our materials built upon linguistic understanding *is the ability to read for meanings.* (p. 244)

A bit of prose is then cited in which 58% of the running words follow regular
spellings:

Nat is a cat.
Nat is fat.
Nat is a fat cat.

A portion of Fries' rationale for meaning follows.

The first sentence specifies the meaning of the word *Nat* by identifying it with the well-
known animal, *cat.* For us this identification is that *Nat* is the cat's name.

Nat is a cat

The second sentence adds to the meaning by asserting that this particular cat, *Nat,* has
a special physical feature to be described as *fat.*

Nat is fat.

The third sentence adds more to the meaning by bringing the description and the identification together in one summary sentence.

Nat is a fat cat.

The three sentences are tied together into a sequence by the repetition of the word
Nat. (p. 246)

This rationale is built on impeccable logic and the application of linguistic principles. Yet one might be pardoned for feeling that this defense of *Nat the fat cat*
represents a victory for meaning that is more apparent than real.

Opposition to Phonics Instruction

Proponents of the regular-spelling approach to reading instruction have voiced criticism of phonics instruction (teaching relationship of letter-sounds). Much of their
opposition is based on two erroneous premises. The first of these is the misconception that the purpose of phonics instruction is to teach the child how to *pronounce*
words by teaching him speech sounds. Bloomfield wrote:

The inventors of these (phonic) methods confuse writing with speech. They plan the
work as though the child were being taught to speak. . . . If a child has not learned to
utter the speech sounds of our language, the only sensible course is to postpone reading until he has learned to speak. As a matter of fact, nearly all six-year-old children

have long ago learned to speak their native language; they have no need whatever of the drill which is given by phonic methods. (p. 27)

This issue was discussed in chapter 1 where it was stated that the purpose of phonics instruction is to teach the child to associate printed letter-symbols with known speech sounds. He does not apply phonic analysis in order to learn *how* to pronounce words. His problem is that he does not know *what spoken word* is represented by a particular pattern of letters. Phonic analysis leads him to this discovery. Only in this sense is phonics related to pronouncing words.

The second misconception about phonics is found in the belief as to how phonics is taught. For example, Bloomfield states:

> The second error of the phonic methods is that of isolating the speech sounds. The authors of these methods tell us to show the child a letter, for instance *t*, and to make him react by uttering the *t*-sound; that is the English speech sound which occurs at the beginning of a word like *two* or *ten*. This sound is to be uttered either all by itself or else with an obscure vowel sound after it. (p. 28)

This description of phonics instruction was valid for an earlier era, but the practice had largely disappeared by the time Bloomfield inveighed against it. It is true that one cannot separately pronounce letter sounds, which taken together constitute the pronunciation of English words, and children are not asked to do so. They are taught that a particular letter represents the same speech sound in many different words, and they are invited to think or subvocalize this sound when the letter occurs in a word they are attempting to solve.

This teaching is not at all inconsistent with linguistic science. For example, linguists agree that the letter *l* has a characteristic identifiable sound in each of the words *l*ake, *l*et, *l*ike, *l*ock, and *l*uck, regardless of which vowel sound follows the *l*. The initial phoneme in each of these words, and thousands of others, would be transcribed /*l*/. In order to crack the code, the beginning reader must come to much the same conclusion as does the linguist.

Code Cracking with a Missing Ingredient

The program offered in *Let's Read* consists of teaching 5,000 words of which only 38% are presented as regular spellings. The first 97 lessons in *Let's Read* introduce words which enjoy regular spellings, while the last 148 lessons present irregular words. The issue of the high number of irregular spellings is raised because Bloomfield's suggestion relative to teaching these irregular words seems totally unrealistic.

Since letter-sound relationships are not taught in the study of regularly spelled words, there can be no transfer of learning from the early instruction to later reading situations. Bloomfield was aware of this, but failed to grasp its significance. He wrote, "There is a great difference between the work of Lessons 1–97 and almost all the child's later work in reading. . . . when it comes to teaching irregular and special words, each word will demand a separate effort and separate practice" (p. 206). Here is the point where this system comes face to face with its inherent weakness. Once the regularly spelled words have been introduced, teaching the balance of English words "demands a separate effort and separate practice." While these are rather vague directions, it is clear that the proponents of the system do not talk in terms of transfer.

Since letter-sound relations are not taught, those children who do not gain insights on their own will have to be taught these relationships before they can make further progress in learning to read.

Beginning Instruction Only, Then . . .

As noted above, once the regularly spelled words are exhausted, teaching irregular words will demand a separate effort and separate practice. No guidelines or blueprint for such instruction are provided. Once again, after an initial instructional blitz designed to get children off to a fast start in reading, they and the teacher are abandoned when the more difficult aspects of learning to read can no longer be avoided.

Programmed Reading

Programmed materials in book form have been developed for teaching a wide assortment of facts, processes, and subject matter. The rationale of programming will not be discussed here other than to mention one of the salient features of this approach. Practically all programmed materials consist of a large series of very small steps on the learning continuum. Each step confronts the learner with a stimulus statement, a problem to be solved, or a relationship to be grasped. She is then immediately tested to see if she has learned what was presented and is informed of her success or failure on the test item. Her responses determine to some degree what her next task will be (i.e., go back and review, do more items of the same nature, or go on to the next step).

Probably the most widely known programmed materials in the area of reading are those developed by Sullivan Associates (distributed by McGraw-Hill Book Co.). These materials consist of a prereading program which serves as a foundation for moving into the actual programmed material. The basic materials consist of 21 conventional sized workbooks which are divided equally between grades one, two, and three. Other supplementary story-type materials have also been developed.

Programmed reading has considerable emphasis on phonics or code cracking. Before a child can actually move into the programmed workbooks there must be considerable progress in letter recognition and in associating printed letters with the speech sounds they represent. The degree to which programmed reading stresses and depends upon phonic analysis is illustrated by the skills a child must have acquired in the prereading stage, such as knowing:

1. the capital and small letters, being able to name these, which of course implies the ability to differentiate between letter forms;
2. how to print both capital and small letters;
3. that groups of letters represent words, that words are read from left to right, and that letters represent speech sounds;
4. the speech sounds which are associated with the letters a, f, m, n, p, t, th, and i;
5. a number of words including yes, no, man, I, ant, mat, a, pin, pan, tan, thin, fat. This prepares the child to read sentences such as I am a man, I am a mat, I am an ant, I am a pin, I am a pan, I am fat, I am thin.

After extensive drill on these skills the child begins work in which pictures provide the stimulus. For example, a picture of a man is used to evoke pupil responses such as the following where the child:

1. circles the naming word(s):
   - man   ant
   - a man   an ant
   - I am a man   I am an ant

2. circles correct response:
   - an ant
   - I am   a man
   - a mat

3. supplies the missing letter: I am a _____an
   - (m_____n)
   - (ma_____)

The tasks related to the picture of *man* are interspersed with the similar use of many other stimulus pictures such as *ant, mat, fan, pan, pin, tan mat, fat man, thin man,* etc.

Programmed reading materials developed thus far appear to be more viable for early instruction than for later stages. When children move into the upper levels covered by the materials, they are expected to read difficult material while still filling in missing letters in words. It is obvious that if they can read the materials then performance of these tasks is no longer relevant to their growth in reading ability.

Words in Color

Words in Color is a beginning reading program developed by Caleb Gattengo (1962). The regular alphabet and traditional spelling of words are retained. However, 39 different colors, each representing a different speech sound, are used in the initial presentation of letters and words. All teaching is done either from the blackboard or from a series of 29 wall charts.

Any letter or combination of letters which represent a given speech sound are shown on the wall charts in the same color. For instance, the long sound of *a* is spelled or represented by *a, ay, eigh, ea, ey, aigh, ei, ai*. These and other letters which represent the long sound of *a* would be colored deep green on the wall charts (or on the blackboard if the teacher elected to print the following words in color): g*a*te, s*ay*, w*eigh*, gr*ea*t, th*ey*, str*aigh*t, th*ei*r, m*ai*l. A lavender color is used to represent the sound of *f* in *fish*, as well as *lf* in ha*lf*, *gh* in cou*gh*, *ff* in pu*ff*, and *ph* in *photograph*.

Initially, children are not taught letter names, but they receive intensive drill on letter-sound associations. The five short vowel sounds are introduced first and are sounded in isolation: *a* = *ah; e* = *eh*, etc. Drill includes printing several vowel letters on the board (a separate color for each). The teacher will then point to or tap each of the letters in the series such as *a-a-e-e-a* to which the class responds "ah-ah-eh-eh-ah." Systematic drill then continues stressing the blending of vowel and consonant letter-sounds to arrive at: "ah + tuh = at."

No Reading Material in Colored Print

One can only imagine how difficult it would be to set even the simplest story in colored print using the *Words in Color* code. There are no sustained reading materials printed in this code. Thus the only colored printing that the child sees are the wall charts, 8 of which contain letter combinations and 21 which contain whole words but no sentences. It is theoretically possible, but not likely, that the teacher will write sustained story or chart material on the board using the color code. Assuming the teacher wished to write *Washington's Birthday,* he would have to assemble 16 different colors of chalk, remembering to use them in the proper sequence.

Since the child reads nothing in color and the large wall code charts are available only in the classroom, it would appear that the more he learned to rely upon the color cues, the less likely it would be that he would ever become an independent reader.

It is very difficult to visualize the use of 39 colors in the spelling of words that children will meet in beginning reading. It is quite likely that some children will develop problems in the discrimination of just noticeable differences in colors such as: cadmium green, yellow green (No. 15), yellow green (No. 47), dark green, olive green, light green, deep green, emerald green (No. 45), emerald green (No. 26), leaf green, gray green, yellow ochre, brown ochre.

Summary

For over a century, criticism of American reading instruction led to changes in materials and methodology that were as predictable as the path of a pendulum. Reformers advocated using more phonics or less phonics instruction, dependent on which of these instructional modes was then in ascendency. However, during the 1950–60s, dissatisfaction with reading instruction reached a new high. A large number of children were not learning to read and an even larger number had unsatisfactory reading achievements.

This happened to coincide with a point on the historical continuum in which the dominant emphasis was on phonics instruction. Defending the status quo was not a viable option. A number of methods-materials were spawned. These were welcomed, not out of malice toward children, but with the hope that the promises accompanying the materials might be an effective panacea.

Some of these materials have been discussed in this chapter. It must be remembered that they were endorsed by experts, hyped in professional journals, and discussed at local, state, and national reading conferences. The materials were treated as being credible simply because there was a need to believe in their value.

In times when reason seems to have been suspended, it is almost impossible to perceive this phenomenon while it is taking place. Hindsight has certain built-in advantages. Some children actually did learn using each material described. Since these materials focused only on *beginning reading,* many were actually able to deliver a "fast start." In so doing, they ignored, postponed, or sidestepped certain essential but difficult tasks that children had to master to become readers of English. The fast start was a false start.

3

Phonics and
Reading Instruction

Educators often have difficulty convincing critics that learning to read and teaching reading are difficult and frustrating experiences. They listen as educators explain that "reading is getting meaning," and readily admit that children come to school with a highly developed mastery of language including a vast array of meanings. Further, during the first two years of reading instruction, children will not be asked to read material that contains concepts beyond their grasp. Then when educators insist that "the school must build on what the child brings to school," it appears that learning to read should be a snap. While reading is getting meaning, *learning to read* is much more!

Children can handle:

"What do these words mean?"

Their problem is:

"What are these words?"

The only solution is learning to identify words. To do this the child must learn the relationship between visual cues (letters) and the speech sounds they represent (phoneme-grapheme relationship). After words have been identified and have been met hundreds of times, they are *recognized*. These words are now known, and no process of identifying them is required. Getting to this level or stage is called *learning to read*. Learning to read is a difficult task *because learning letter-sound relationships is totally foreign to any of the child's previous experiences.*

How Children Learn to Read

Learning to read is a complicated, long-term process. Few adults can recall significant details of how they learned to read. If we observe someone *teaching* a child to read, we are seeing a very small segment of instruction. Every observation would focus on the teaching of a particular skill. Observing the teacher, the materials, and the methodology, however, would not reveal what is taking place within the learner. If we observe the learner, we are limited to a number of overt behaviors from which we hypothesize what mental processes are at work.

Assume that on the first day of school, the first grade teacher points to a word in a story and asks a nonreader, "What is this word?" Obviously, the child cannot answer. If the teacher says, "I will read you the sentence leaving out that word. Listen carefully and then tell me the word." She reads, "The teacher asked the new girl, 'What is your _____?' " Probably 95% of first grade nonreaders could supply the missing word. This illustrates what the nonreader brings to school that relates to reading. The child is adequately equipped to deal with the language-meaning aspect of reading. But he cannot begin with the magic of language until he has established what words these strange symbols represent.

After a few weeks of "learning to read," the children will have changed drastically. For example, a child is reading a story that contains fewer than a dozen different words. The reader does not recognize the word *man* in the sentence *the man is sad.* The teacher suggests "Sound it out." The child instantly responds "Boy."

The peculiar thing about this situation is that the child heard the teacher and had the ability to do what was suggested. However, the pupil had already settled on a response that had worked before—guessing. In recent reading experiences, the child had met many words he did not instantly recognize and at various times had tried all the following responses:

- Skipping the word
- Asking someone for help (teacher, parent, peer)
- Ignoring all phonic clues and guessing the word
   (bad guess—makes no sense—now sounds out)
   (good guess—correct word—reinforces guessing)
- Applying phonics to sound out word
- Sounding out first letter and instantly guessing the word
   (saying wrong word—it makes sense—no problem)
   (saying wrong word—it makes sense—big problem, because the substitute word demands changes later in the paragraph in order to keep the meaning)
- Trying to apply phonics, which doesn't work on the irregularly spelled word *once*; falls back on context clues, solves word

Ad infinitum. . . .

It is apparent that the beginning reader has many available options for solving unknown words. Some of these are very poor responses, but unfortunately, even the poorest are reinforced occasionally. Learning to read involves discarding ineffective responses and using *all* available clues that make for success. To make reasonable progress, the beginning reader must acquire three closely related skills:

- mastering and applying letter-sound relationships
- enlarging sight vocabulary
- profiting from context clues while reading

Beginning reading instruction is so important because it is here that children develop a sense of what reading is. It is not good instruction to devote the first few months of reading to one of the above skills while ignoring the other two. This kind of approach will confuse a child regarding the true nature of the reading process. An extensive time block devoted to phonics instruction leads the child to view reading as sounding out words. On the other hand, a lengthy instructional period without insight into letter-sound relationships leads a child to see reading as a process in which you guess at words you don't know. Serious damage to the learner can result from either set. Early instruction should help learners develop the insight that these three skills complement each other in helping to crack the two codes—word identification and meaning. The only way children can miss the fact that reading is a meaning-making process is to receive instruction that masks this fact.

Obviously essential to reading is *cracking the code,* learning to associate printed letters with the speech sounds they represent. Everything in spoken English can be printed using only 26 different letter symbols. This is possible because, in general, letters and letter-combinations stand for the same speech sounds in thousands of different words. Despite the fact that there is not a one-to-one correspondence between letter(s) seen and speech sounds represented, learning to read depends on mastery of the symbol-sound relationship.

To illustrate how phonics works, we will focus on what the child gains by learning one letter-sound relationship. (Teaching letter-sound relationships is discussed in later chapters.) Here we will simply assume that the child has been taught to:

1. visually recognize the letter form *m,* and
2. associate *m* with the sound it represents at the beginning of words such as *man, my, met.*

Of course, before coming to school, children have mastered several important related skills.

They can make the *m* sound in hundreds of spoken words.

They can differentiate this sound in all of the words (language) they hear. In listening to speech they do not confuse the word *man* with the words can, pan, fan, ran, tan—even though the difference in the sound of these words is minimal.

Phonics instruction invites the child to internalize the following (in his own language):

When I see the letter *m* I think of the sound it represents. This is the first sound in the familiar words, *me, my.*

Any unknown word I meet that begins with *m* starts with the same sound as *me, my.*

The unknown word *man* cannot be *boy—cat—girl*; or *pan—ran—fan.* The correct word *must* begin like *me* and *my.* Next, teaching will focus on the sounds represented by medial vowels and final consonants. Each step mastered provides a bit more independence in reading.

The most frustrating aspect of teaching reading is that instruction cannot focus directly and exclusively on what children already know—the meanings imbedded in what they are asked to read. The intervening step of discovering the identity of the words is what complicates the procedures of learning to read. These procedures can take a lot of the joy out of learning. As Jerome Bruner once said to reading teachers, "The act of *learning* to read is not a self-sustaining activity." This is difficult for avid readers to understand since for them reading is a self-sustaining activity.

The problem stems from our reluctance to accept the fact that there is little in common between learning to read and skillful reading. The expert and the learner may be on the same learning continuum, but they are not engaged in the same activity.

Despite the difficulties in learning to read, there is no cause for despair. We must remember that when a child meets an unknown word, whatever it is that goes through her mind is handled much faster than any discussion of this phenomenon. Every gain a child makes in learning to read will transfer to future learning situations. For instance, after several weeks of instruction, she will have met some words so frequently that she will recognize them instantly. Once this happens she will never again puzzle over the speech sounds represented by individual letters in these words.

Soon the reader is able to deal with sentences and larger units of print. The fact that reading must follow the rules of speech is now a tremendous asset to the beginning reader. This is where the child is quite proficient; many reading "errors" become self-correcting. Instruction can now build on what the child knows. We will see how some specific learnings can inhibit growth while others provide insights and momentum in the learning-to-read process.

Overview of Word Analysis Skills

We have already listed a number of responses that children might use when they read unknown words. In the literature on reading, these attempts to solve unknown words have been discussed under headings such as *word attack skills, word analysis skills,* or *word identification skills.* These are the major approaches one might use to identify unknown words:

- unique letter or word configuration clues
- picture clues
- phonic analysis
- structural analysis
- context clues

Word Form (Unique Letter Configuration)

This is the least useful of the various clues available for solving unknown words. It is doubtful that there is any value in teaching children to look for odd or striking visual letter patterns. It is probable, however, that some children will note certain of these on their own. In general, all words (except homographs: *wind-wind; lead-lead,* etc.) can be said to be unique in appearance. Yet, in the experience of a primary-level child, the visual forms of words are so much alike that much practice is needed to perceive the minute differences between them. While learning to discriminate word forms, the child might note such limited factors as the length of words or special features such as *tt, ll, oo,* or final *y.* Learning to recognize the word *monkey* because it has a tail (*y*) at the end may serve an immediate and limited purpose, but soon the child will meet *money, merry, funny,* and *penny.* The word *look* may be learned as having two eyes in the middle, but soon the child meets *book, stood, flood.* It is obvious that, as the child expands her reading, these unique features are found in a large number of words and thus become of less and less value in identifying different words.

Picture Clues

Certain critics oppose the use of pictures in early reading materials on the basis that some children will rely too heavily on pictures. If this occurs, it interferes with learning to read. Those critical of using pictures often advocate approaches that emphasize code cracking in beginning reading. Materials of this nature do not usually lend themselves to very meaningful illustrations.

It is true that pictures may provide clues to unknown words (*turkey, cliff, wagon, father, bridge, fireplace*). Pictures may suggest words. In addition, they also have high motivational value and will often lure a young reader into reading. Pictures help focus attention on meaning; they lead into a story, and where only a limited number of words are known, pictures supplement. They serve as stimuli for oral language use in group discussions.

When children are observed to overrely on picture clues, this observation should have diagnostic significance for the teacher. It suggests that certain instructional practices may need closer examination, rather than that pictures should be proscribed in children's reading materials.

Phonic Analysis

Phonic analysis, or "cracking the code," has been defined and discussed; here we will limit restatements to three sentences that summarize what it is, what it does, and what it isn't. Phonics instruction *is* teaching letter-sound relationships. Its *purpose* is to provide beginning readers with a means of identifying unknown printed words. Phonics *is not* a method of teaching reading, but is an essential ingredient of reading instruction.

Structural Analysis

Structural analysis deals with one of the most important cue systems available to children learning to read. Root words are among the first words children learn (*look, call, fill, move, stop, need*). In English writing there are a large number of prefabricated, highly consistent spelling patterns that are added to thousands of root words; for example, prefixes such as *un—re—dis—pre—con—in;* inflectional endings, *s—ed—ing;* and suffixes, *ment—tive—ly—less—able.*

Profiting from structural analysis instruction depends to some degree on previous learnings. If the child is familiar with the word *fill,* he may have little trouble identifying, *refill,* or even *refillable,* although affixes completely surround the root word.

Beginning readers need to develop awareness of the visual changes produced in words by:

Adding affixes

Combining two words to form compounds (*anyone, somewhere*)

Writing plurals (*s — es — ies*)

Forming contractions (*can't, I'll, doesn't, I've*)

Context Clues

When a child is reading for meaning, the context in which she meets an unknown word is useful in suggesting what the word might be. Usually, only a few words could possibly fill out the meaning; for example:

The boy threw the ball to his _____.

Probably fewer than a dozen words could logically be inserted in the blank space (*friend, dog, mother, playmate, sister, father, brother*). Some possibilities would be less logical than others depending on what has happened in the story prior to this sentence.

Authors use a number of devices to provide context clues that help readers solve new words and difficult concepts. One of these is to incorporate a description-definition in the text:

They were now traveling through _____ country. It was very hot, there was sand underfoot and the wind blew sand in their eyes. There were no streams — no water whatsoever — and no shade trees. The _____ extended as far as the eye could see.

Other techniques include comparison or contrast and the use of synonyms or antonyms:

At this point the stream flowed very _____ [rapidly]. The water splashed over the rocks and sent up white spray as it moved swiftly through the pass.

Solving the identity of an unknown word is facilitated by (a) the meaning of the total sentence in which the word occurs, and (b) what has occurred in previously read sentences and sentences that follow — assuming, of course, that the child is reading for meaning.

Skills in Combination

The approaches to word analysis that we have described are probably not of equal value in learning to read. Different children may learn to rely on one method more than on others, and some approaches, such as unique word form, have limited utility beyond the early stages of learning to read. Facile reading would not result if one went through a series of trial-and-error responses using only one of the preceding approaches to word analysis. Efficient readers use various methods of word attack simultaneously.

Seeing phonics in proper perspective involves: (a) understanding that phonic analysis is one means by which children can solve words not known as sight words; (b) noting that phonics relates to, and interacts with, all the other methods of word analysis. For example, structural and phonic analysis constantly interact. Such pre-fabricated units as *ex-, pre-, dis-, en-, pro-, -ed, -ing, -tive, -ment, -tion,* when added to words, do produce structural changes. Each of these, and many more, are also phonic units. The pronunciation of prefixes, suffixes, and compound words remains quite consistent.

Structural changes in a word will often camouflage clues the reader might have used in recognizing the root. When a child does not instantly recognize such a new word, he should resort to sounding. For example, a child may know the word *locate,* but not recognize *dislocated* or *relocating.* Sounding the parts will unlock the pronunciation and, since the meaning of the root word is known, the meaning of the new word is grasped. A child should not be taught to rely exclusively on one method or approach for solving unknown words. In the incomplete sentence under "Context Clues," we noted that the context permits several logical choices:

The boy threw the ball to his _____.

Here the reader is restricted to context alone. But with good instruction he will learn not to rely exclusively on context clues. In addition, in an actual reading situation he would not be confronted with a blank space, but rather a series of letters. Notice that when the reader heeds the initial letter and solves the sound it represents, the number of logical choices is drastically reduced:

The boy threw the ball to his s_____.

It is doubtful the reader will need more than the minimal clue provided, but if the reader needs to, he may sound and blend more of the letters—sis_____.

Context clues are not limited to the sentence in which the unknown word occurs. For example, assume a child is reading the following sentence in which the blank represents an unknown word:

A. "Look," said Jack, "look at the _____."

The context of example A alone does not provide enough context clues for the reader to solve the unknown word. In example B, the sentence appears in a larger context:

B. "I hear a car," said Jack.
"I do not hear a car," said Suzy. "I hear a funny noise."
"I hear a honk-honk," said Jack, "but I do not see a car."
"That noise is in the sky," said Suzy.
Jack pointed at the sky. "Look," said Jack.
"Look at the g_____." Suzy said, "They are flying south for the winter."

At this point, some readers' background and previous experience will suggest the unknown word. The context suggests several classes of subjects, such as birds or airplanes, which would be logical. In the child's book, however, the unknown is not a blank space, but a word composed of letters. The sounds these letters represent have been studied. Even though the word is not known, the child who has been properly taught will note the initial consonant *g.* He will not say *bird* or *airplane* or any other word that does not begin with the *g* sound. He will sound as much as he needs:

Look at the g_____.
gee_____.
geese.

This story, since it is at the primary level, is accompanied by a picture that shows both children looking up, with Jack pointing toward the sky to a V-formation of geese. Thus, context, previous experience, a picture, sounding the initial consonant, then the double vowel, if needed, all provide clues to help the reader solve the unknown word without a noticeable hesitation. The less facile reader might require a pause in her reading while she sounds out the word. Only a very inefficient reader would have to depend entirely on "sounding out" every letter in the unknown word, which would involve wasting all the other clues.

Instructional Issues in Phonics Instruction

Phonics instruction has always been surrounded by controversy, and past and present debate has failed to settle many of the issues. A few examples of questions raised over the years are: Are phonics skills essential for learning to read? If so, how much skill is needed? When should phonics instruction be introduced? In what sequence should skills be learned? Should children be taught phonics "rules"? Is phonics instruction an "additive" to beginning instruction or an integral part of it? What is the best "methodology" for teaching letter-sound relationships: Teaching sounds in isolation? Blending sounds in words? Using substitute alphabets? Diacritical marks? Whole-word regular spelling patterns? Programming the steps? Systematic or incidental instruction? Does phonics instruction produce slow readers who are unconcerned with "meaning"? Is the teaching of phonics and sight words compatible—or antithetical? Since expert readers can't be detected using phonics, why should beginners be burdened with it? Let us touch on a number of these instructional issues.

Is the Mastery of Phonics Skills Essential for Learning to Read?

This is really the issue that has nurtured the phonics vs. sight-word controversy for more than a century. The major premise of this book is that beginning readers who do not learn and apply the letter-sound code can progress only so far in learning to read. It would be futile to attempt to say exactly how far each child can go in terms of words he can learn in the absence of phonics skills. It is fairly safe to say, however, that no child will function as a fluent reader, or even as an average third grade reader, if he does not learn to apply letter-sound relationships in his reading.

It is also safe to say that if a learner progresses in beginning reading without applying the letter-sound code, he will spend more time reading less material. The reason is obvious to the person who has worked with individuals who are learning to read. The terms "learning to read" and "beginning readers" imply limited experience with the written symbol system. The beginning reader faces the burden of making many visual discriminations among printed words that contain only minimal differences in visual cues. Unless letter-sound clues are added, the visual discrimination circuit overloads, and the reading process breaks down.

Why Teach Phonics in Beginning Reading?

Psycholinguists and other theorists have observed that expert readers rely very little, if at all, on letter-sound relationships. They obviously pay no heed to individual letters and cannot be observed applying phonics skills.

A potentially dangerous generalization is that since skilled readers do not appear to use phonics, perhaps children learning how to read need not be taught letter-sound relationships. If such a hypothesis is advanced, it should be accompanied by a description of how the learner will *learn* to read. One suggestion is that possibly "memory" for word forms (that is, visual memory) may be all that is really needed. Smith (1973) writes:

> We can both recognize and recall many thousands of words in our spoken language vocabulary, and recognize many thousands of different faces and animals and plants and objects in our visual world. *Why should this fantastic memorizing capacity suddenly run out in the case of reading?* (p. 75)

Smith does not come out flatly against phonics instruction; however, the question he raises seems to invite the conclusion that visual memory of word configurations should be sufficient for learning to read. If this point of view gains adherents, we shall have come back full circle to the sight-word versus phonics debate. This debate should not be reopened without evidence that children can learn to read without applying letter-sound relationships in the beginning reading stage.

As we try to solve the mystery of how children learn to read, we must not observe experts and generalize to beginners. There are no experts who failed to learn and apply letter-sound relationships, and there are no experts who continue to use phonic clues as they did as beginners. Being expert readers precludes this behavior.

What Is the Optimum Amount of Phonics for a Given Child?

The optimum amount of phonics instruction a child should receive is the minimum amount she needs to become an independent reader. To provide less instruction than a child needs would deny her the opportunity to master a skill she must have to progress in independent reading. To subject children to drill they do not need runs the risk of destroying interest in the act of reading. It is easy to turn off a potential learner by requiring that she sit through group drill on sounding letters or complete a series of workbook pages that force her to deal with minute details of word attack when she is already capable of applying these skills in sustained reading.

The key to providing children with what they need in the way of instruction is knowledge of their weaknesses. We acquire this knowledge through diagnosis. The best diagnosis is observation and analysis of reading behavior. Discovering what a child needs in the area of code-cracking ability should be relatively easy, since she cannot help but disclose her needs. Every technique she might use to cover her weakness is an added clue.

When beginning readers omit, miscall, or substitute words, one tries to find out why. Miscues that do not distort meaning become of minor importance only after a child demonstrates that she can read.

Listening to a child read a sentence or two should provide the teacher with clues to her word attack ability. A hypothesis that a particular skill is lacking can be tested by having the child read words or sentences containing words that call for her to make the letter-sound relationships that fit the hypothesis. If this simple, informal test discloses a problem, the teacher selects or develops appropriate materials and works simultaneously with all pupils who can profit from the instruction decided upon.

What we know about children and how they learn would dictate that we accept the premise that all children in a given classroom do not need identical amounts of phonics instruction. Most phonics instruction materials do not make provision for pupil differences. Differentiation of instruction in this area is primarily the task of the teacher, just as it is in all areas of the curriculum.

Is It Possible to Teach Children to Overrely on Phonic Analysis?

Children can be taught to overrely on phonics (or on sight words, or on guessing from context). Overreliance on any one skill is bad for learners because they inevitably fail to utilize all the available cues. Thus, flexibility and efficiency are diminished.

The beginning reader should be receiving instruction that helps him crack the code, but he is handicapped if he relies too heavily on phonic analysis. If a child can and does sound out every word in a story, he is not becoming an efficient reader. He is analyzing some words long after he should have mastered them as sight words; that is, he may be sounding words the tenth, twentieth, or fiftieth time he meets them. Since the objective of reading instruction is not to produce this kind of reader, every effort should be made to see that the child does not generalize that sounding out words is reading.

Should Children Still Be Taught Sight Words in Beginning Reading?

Starting from the premise that a child must learn to associate printed letter symbols with speech sounds does not negate the fact that one must also learn to recognize whole words. Whenever a child is making normal progress in learning to read, she is increasing her sight vocabulary or stock of words she recognizes instantly. At the end of first grade she will have a larger sight vocabulary than at the end of 5 months of instruction and practice. At the conclusion of second grade, her sight vocabulary will be much larger than it was at the beginning of that school year. The skill that best illustrates the developmental nature of reading is acquisition of a sight vocabulary. When a reader meets words she recognizes, she does not apply phonic analysis. She knows what spoken word the printed form represents; therefore, there is nothing to solve through letter-sound analysis.

Also, the irregular spellings of many English words limit the effectiveness of phonic analysis and dictate these words be learned as sight words (*know, once, head, give, great, have, many, love, does, one, done, here, of, said, too, use, very, gone, should, who, some, put, move, none, son, two*). In addition, a number of words appear so frequently in English speech and writing that it would be wasteful to sound out those words each time they are met. For example, after only a few weeks of reading instruction centering on normal English usage, a child will have met each of the following words often: *can, made, say, stop, keep, like, not, man, sun, make, run, at, bring,* etc.

Principles to Apply in Teaching Phonics

The systematic study of any teaching-learning situation may be expected to yield a set of psychologically sound principles that relate to and govern teaching procedures. In teaching, one would follow sound principles so as to enhance learning. Principles do not spell out precise practices to follow, but rather they provide a set of guidelines by which to measure classroom instructional practices. The following principles for teaching phonic analysis are offered for teachers' consideration. If these principles are found to be educationally sound, they merit application in the classroom.

- *For any child to profit from systematic phonics instruction, he must be able to differentiate among different speech sounds in words and visually discriminate between printed letters.* The absence of either of these prerequisites would preclude learning letter-sound relationships. For example, a child who can differentiate between the sounds of *bee* and *dee* but cannot visually discriminate between the printed symbols *b* and *d* cannot apply phonics in a reading situation involving words that contain these symbols.
- *Practices followed in beginning reading DO tend to inculcate a set in the learner.* Instruction should not lead the child to think of reading as consisting of either learning sight words or sounding letters or relying on context clues. Such instruction is likely to result in overreliance on one or another of these essential skills.
- *Instructional practices should ensure that beginning readers learn all essential word identification skills.* Overreliance on any one skill can impair reading efficiency.
- *All necessary phonic skills (letter-sound relationships) the child needs to become an independent reader should be taught.*
- *All elementary teachers should be familiar with the entire phonics program.* All teachers of reading, regardless of grade level, will probably find it necessary to teach, review, or reteach certain phonic skills to some children in their classrooms. Thus, familiarity with all steps in phonics instruction is essential.
- *Diagnosis is essential for discovering each child's present needs, and diagnosis is the basis for differentiation of instruction.*
- *The spelling patterns in English writing limit the usefulness of certain rules or generalizations.* Little value may reside in teaching a generalization that applies to only a few words or that has numerous exceptions.

Summary

Beginning readers must master letter-sound relationships and apply this knowledge as they learn to read. To become facile readers, children must use ALL word identification skills. However, overreliance on any one skill such as learning sight words, use of context clues, or applying phonic analysis, can interfere with growth in reading ability. The optimum amount of phonics for every child is the minimum that child needs to become an independent reader.

4

Prerequisites for Phonics Instruction

Visual Discrimination

Children will have had innumerable experiences in making visual discriminations before they enter school and are called upon to make the much finer discriminations required in reading. The school will then provide many readiness activities that foster visual discrimination. Some of these may be only vaguely related to learning to read—matching objects and geometric forms, noting missing parts of pictures, and the like.

Other activities will relate more closely to the tasks required in reading. Studies have established that the ability to name the letters of the alphabet is one of the best predictors of a child's success in beginning reading. However, naming letters is a memory-association skill and is really not the crucial issue. The importance of being able to name letters is that it establishes that the child can discriminate visually among the various letter forms. Children have an almost uncanny ability to learn names or labels. Thus, teaching letter names is not the primary goal, but this ability is the criterion for establishing visual discrimination of graphic forms.

Exercises: Matching and Naming Letter Forms

1. Duplicate exercises similar to the illustration. The child circles or traces each letter on the line that is exactly like the stimulus on the left.

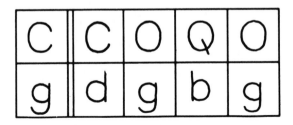

2. Flash Card Drill
    a. Prepare large flash cards for each letter of the alphabet. Hold up a card and select a volunteer to name the letter or have the group name the letter in unison.

    b. Prepare smaller letter-cards for each participant with same letter form on front and back of card.

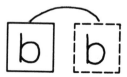

    Hand out identical card groups of 3 or 4 to each participant who spreads cards on desk. Give directions: "Hold up the letter m, . . .," etc. (Observe children having difficulty and provide added practice for these pupils.)
3. Build a Pile
    a. This is a game for two or more children. Use a pack of letter cards, each of which has a letter form on one side only.
    b. The cards are placed face down and the first player draws a card. He shows the card, and if he names the letter he places it face down in his "pile."
    c. When a player fails to name the letter, the next player may try to name it and place it in his "pile." Then he draws a card.
    d. At the end of the game, the player with the most cards in his pile wins.
4. Two-letter Sequence
    Duplicate a series of two-letter words. Instruct children to circle each word that is exactly like the stimulus at the left.

it		at	in	up	it
on		of	on	no	on
is		as	us	is	so

5. Three-letter Sequence (for added difficulty; same instructions as two-letter sequences using three-letter words)

sat		hat	sat	say	sad
can		cat	pan	can	cap
dug		dug	bug	dog	dug

6. Spin a Letter
Prepare a spinner card as in the illustration.

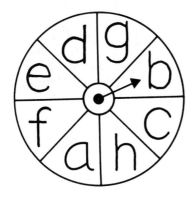

First player spins. If he can name the letter indicated by the spinner, he takes a button or cardboard square from the "bank" and places it in front of him. Next player spins, etc. Player with largest number of markers wins the game. (Prepare several sets of letters to place on the face of spinner card.)

Variations:
   a. One child spins and calls on another player to "name the letter." If the child called on identifies the letter, he then spins and calls on another child to "name the letter."
   b. Prepare capital letters printed on cardboard squares for each lowercase letter on the spinner dial. First player draws a capital letter form and selects another child to move the spinner to the corresponding lowercase letter on the wheel. If successful, she draws a capital letter and selects a new player to move the spinner.

Exercises: Matching Capital and Lowercase Letters

1. Child draws a line from capital letter at left of box to lowercase letter at right of box.

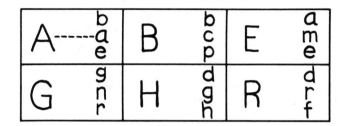

2. Duplicate a page of boxes, each box containing two letter forms. The child circles each pair of letters that contains both a capital and lowercase form of the same letter.

Hh	Ee	Fg	Bb
Ba	Gg	Dd	Aa

3. Prepare a series of cards similar to examples. (Each participant has lowercase letter cards for each letter in exercise.) Place one capital letter form on chalk tray. Call on volunteer to place lowercase letter below capital forms shown. Continue through cards.

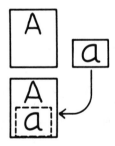

4. Tic-Tac-Toe
   a. Duplicate pages of 3″ × 3″ squares.
   b. Each set has a capital letter in the center square and a variety of lowercase letters in all other squares. These should be arranged so that one line contains the capital and two lowercase forms of the same letter.
   c. Have the child draw a line through the three squares that contain the same letter form.

a	o	a
a	A	c
e	a	a

a	c	o
e	E	a
o	c	e

g	b	p
b	B	b
p	d	b

5. Jigsaw Matching
   a. Prepare a number of cards, each containing a capital and matching lowercase letter form.

   b. Cut cards as indicated along dotted line and shuffle pieces.
   c. Child matches capital and lowercase letters. (Different jigsaw cuts permit matching even if child does not know both letter forms.)
   d. Variation for added difficulty: Make the same "cut" on a series of cards. Here the child receives no clue from the shape of the pieces.

Exercises: Tracing Letter Forms

1. Print large letter form on chalkboard. Trace the form and say letter name while children trace the form in the air and give letter name.
2. Prepare duplicated pages showing heavy-line letter form on left and dotted letter outlines on balance of line. Children trace over the dots to form the letters.

3. Duplicate a page of letter stimuli as shown. The child traces each letter outline that will result in the same letter as the stimulus at the left.

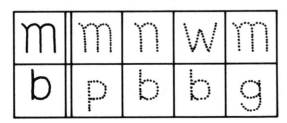

4. After tracing the first letter outlined, the child prints the letter in each of the remaining boxes on the line.

5. Complete the Letter
Prepare a page of letter symbols, each of which is followed by a partially completed letter. The child is to add the part that is missing in order to complete the model shown at the left.

Examples:

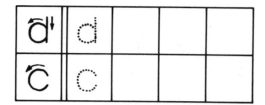

 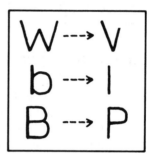 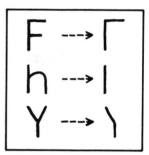

Exercise: Discrimination of Word Forms

In this task, the child does not have to be able to name the words; the child simply underlines every word in the box that is the same as the stimulus word at the left. Exercises progress from gross differences to minimum differences.

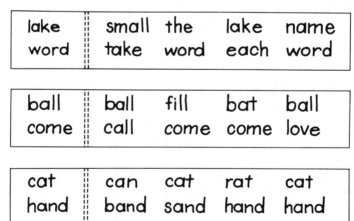

Auditory Discrimination

Learning to read involves both the ability to make finer and finer visual discriminations between printed word symbols and the ability to associate oral speech sounds with printed letters and letter combinations. These are often referred to as *mechanical skills,* whose value is sometimes downgraded in comparison with the so-called higher-level comprehension skills. It is a mistake to argue the relative virtues of decoding and comprehension in beginning reading, since both are absolutely essential ingredients in the process of learning to read.

Phonics instruction is related to previous learnings. Prior to reading, children have had many auditory experiences with language that bear directly on learning to read. Upon entering school, children:

Can differentiate between thousands of words spoken by other individuals

Can use thousands of words in their own speech

Have developed concepts for thousands of words

Successfully teaching all subsequent steps in phonic analysis is based on the child's ability to discriminate between speech sounds in words. The ability to make or use all English speech sounds in words does not assure the ability to discriminate between individual phonemes in words. Children learn spoken words as global units and can easily distinguish between words with minimal phoneme differences. Phonics instruction aims at instant association of a particular sound with a given letter or letters. Thus, if a child cannot distinguish the minute auditory differences being taught in a particular phonics lesson, she cannot profit from that instruction.

Occasionally, children are fairly successful in learning consonant sounds but have trouble mastering certain vowel sounds. An example of such a case is a high school student who could not differentiate between spoken words containing the short sound of *e* or *i.* Pairs of words, which differed only as to the vowel in medial position, were numbered for identification purposes. The tutor would say one of the words and ask the boy to give the number of the word pronounced. His responses demonstrated conclusively that he could not aurally distinguish between words such as the following:

A.	(1) bet	(2) bit	**D.**	(1) pen	(2) pin
B.	(1) Ben	(2) bin	**E.**	(1) bed	(2) bid
C.	(1) mitt	(2) met	**F.**	(1) then	(2) thin

Many hours of practice were required for the boy to overcome this deficiency. A tape recorder was used as the tutor and the boy read words from identical lists. The tutor would pronounce a word, then the boy would say the same word using the tutor's pronunciation as a model. The student listened to the recordings many times before he was able to differentiate between these vowel sounds.

A learning problem like this could develop because the student could correctly pronounce the words he used in his speech, and he always had context clues when others used words that contained the troublesome sounds. Probably none of his teachers were aware that he persisted in hearing many words or syllables globally rather than clearly distinguishing component phonemes. To illustrate, if someone clearly spoke the sentence, ''The pig is in the PEG PIN,'' he would be under the impression he had heard, ''The pig is in the *pig pen*'' because the context seemed to demand this.

Initial Sounds in Words

The procedures a teacher might use to help children develop skill in auditory discrimination are practically unlimited. The following are illustrative.

1. Children listen while the teacher pronounces a series of words, all of which begin with the same consonant sound: *b*elt, *b*all, *b*ird, *b*e, *b*one. Children then volunteer other words that begin with the same sound: *b*aby, *b*ug, *b*at, *b*oom, *b*ang.
2. Grouping pairs of pictures by initial sound.
   Collect a number of pictures from workbooks, catalogues, or magazines. Paste each picture on a separate piece of cardboard to make handling easier. Select several pairs of pictures whose naming words begin with the same sound. The child then groups these according to initial sound (ball-boat; house-horse; fence-feather; pig-pumpkin; log-ladder; etc.).

As the children progress, the difficulty level of the exercise can be increased by including three or more pictures whose names begin with the same sound.

Exercises: Initial Sounds

1. Secure pictures that contain many objects (advertisements, etc.).
   Teacher: ''Do you see an object that begins with the sound we hear at the beginning of the names Billy and Betty?'' (ball—basket)
   ''Do you see a picture of something that begins with the sound we hear at the beginning of the words hand and help?'' (hat—horse)
   Continue to use stimulus words whose initial sound matches that of naming words for objects pictured.

2. Picture Strips
   Prepare a series of picture strips, each containing a stimulus picture at the left and three or four other pictures. The child names a picture only if its name begins with the same sound as the model at the left. (Note: Always identify picture names before children work independently, to avoid the confusion of calling a pail a bucket or a fox a dog, and so on.)

Exercises: Working with Rhymes

The purpose of the following activities is to provide practice in discriminating speech sounds in words, specifically rhyming elements. In addition the exercises focus on developing other skills such as: (a) listening (limiting responses to one category—numbers, colors, animals); (b) following directions; (c) noting stress and intonation patterns.

1. Matching Rhyming Picture Names
    Place on the bulletin board, flannel board, or chalk tray a number of "pairs" of pictures whose naming words rhyme. (Mix the pictures.) Children volunteer to remove two pictures whose naming words rhyme. The child then names the pictures:

    "This is a dog.
    This is a log.
    Dog and log rhyme."

2. Thinking of Rhyming Words
    Explain that sentences will be read. Children are to listen carefully so they can supply words that rhyme with the last word in each sentence. (Note: The last word in the sentence is stressed; in some classroom situations it may be advisable to repeat it once.)

    1. Be sure to wear a hat on your *head.* (red, bed, Ted, said)
    2. We will take a trip to the *lake.*
    3. John, you may pet the *cat.*

4. They all said hello to the *man.*
5. Have you ever seen a *moose?*
6. We watched the bird build its *nest.*
7. Let's all count to *ten.*
8. Mary walked in the rain and got *wet.*
9. Sunday, we went to the *beach.*

Variation:
Prepare sentences in which the final word is omitted. In reading the sentence, one word is emphasized. The child completes the sentence by giving a word that rhymes with the word that is emphasized. This procedure also teaches the concept of *stress* as part of intonation patterns.

1. A *frog* sat on a _____. (log)
2. Mary will *bake* a chocolate _____. (cake)
3. Please do not bounce the *ball* in the _____. (hall)
4. On his finger the *king* wore a _____. (ring)
5. *Kate* will *wait* by the _____. (gate)
6. Keith swept the *room* with a nice new _____. (broom)

3. Number Rhymes
Explain the activity—that the teacher will pronounce and emphasize two words that rhyme with a number-word. The children are to supply the rhyming number word to finish each sentence.

1. *Blue* and *shoe* rhyme with _____. (two)
2. *Gate* and *hate* rhyme with _____. (eight)
3. *Fix* and *mix* rhyme with _____. (six)
4. *Drive* and *hive* rhyme with _____. (five)
5. *Gun* and *run* rhyme with _____. (one)
6. *Tree* and *see* rhyme with _____. (three)
7. *When* and *then* rhyme with _____. (ten)
8. *Pine* and *line* rhyme with _____. (nine)
9. *Door* and *more* rhyme with _____. (four)
10. *Eleven* and *heaven* rhyme with _____. (seven)

To provide practice in speaking in sentences, have one volunteer say the entire sentence after each rhyme: "*Gate* and *late* rhyme with *eight.*"
    Variation: This activity is similar except that the last word the teacher speaks is the clue to the rhyming word. Teacher: "Give me a number that rhymes with _____."

1. fun (*one*)		6. hen (*ten*)	
2. fix (*six*)		7. late (*eight*)	
3. fine (*nine*)		8. do (*two*)	
4. floor (*four*)		9. alive (*five*)	
5. bee (*three*)		10. heaven (*seven*)	

4. Color Names to Complete a Rhyme
   Teacher: "Name the color that rhymes with _____."

   1. *head* and *bed* _____. (*red*)
   2. *clean* and *queen* _____. (*green*)
   3. *tray* and *play* _____. (*gray*)
   4. *do* and *you* _____. (*blue*)
   5. *track* and *back* _____. (*black*)
   6. *town* and *gown* _____. (*brown*)
   7. *man* and *ran* _____. (*tan*)
   8. *sight* and *kite* _____. (*white*)
   9. *think* and *sink* _____. (*pink*)
   10. *fellow* and *Jello* _____. (*yellow*)

5. Animal Names to Complete a Rhyme
   Teacher: "Name an animal that rhymes with _____."

   1. *hat* _____. (rat, cat)   6. *near* _____. (deer)
   2. *log* _____. (dog, frog)   7. *Jeep* _____. (sheep)
   3. *house* _____. (mouse)   8. *cantaloupe* _____. (antelope)
   4. *boat* _____. (goat)   9. *big* _____. (pig)
   5. *mitten* _____. (kitten)   10. *box* _____. (fox)

6. Rhyming Words and Following Directions
   Each participant should have two 3" × 5" cards with the word YES printed on both sides of one card, and NO on both sides of the other.
   The teacher reads statements similar to those below. If the two emphasized words rhyme, children hold up the YES card; if the words do not rhyme, they hold up the NO card.

   1. I say *fox* and *box*. (yes)
   2. I say *coat* and *road*. (no)
   3. I say *found* and *ground*. (yes)
   4. I say *man* and *men*. (no)
   5. I say *car* and *cart*. (no)
   6. I say *feet* and *meet*. (yes)
   7. I say *book* and *look*. (yes)
   8. I say *glass* and *dress*. (no)
   9. I say *bug* and *rug*. (yes)
   10. I say *chair* and *church*. (no)

7. Forming Rhymes with Letter Names
   Teacher: "Name a letter(s) that rhymes with _____." or "What let-
             ter(s) rhymes with _____?"

   1. *say* and *day*? (a, k, j)
   2. *me* and *tree*? (b, c, d, e, g, v, t, z, p)
   3. *sell* and *bell*?(l)
   4. *hen* and *ten*? (n)

    5. *high* and *sky?* (i, y)
    6. *far* and *car?* (r)
    7. *true* and *blue?* (u, q)
    8. *them* and *gem?* (m)
    9. *no* and *grow?* (o)
    10. *dress* and *less?* (s)

8. Picture Rhymes
Duplicate a series of boxes, each containing either three or four pictures. Select pictures so that two naming words rhyme. The child is to draw a line connecting these two pictures.
Teacher: "Name the pictures. Two will rhyme. Connect these pictures every time."

Final Sounds in Words

Besides practice on initial sounds and rhyming elements, the child needs auditory practice in matching and differentiating the final sound in words (nonrhyming elements). It is easier for the child to note that *cat* and *rat* end with the same *sounds* than it is to note that *cat* and *tent* end with the same *sound*.

    Drill and practice on final sounds can be provided by adapting procedures and approaches cited earlier, as well as with the following exercises.

Exercises: Final Sounds

1. Oral Practice
Explain that you will pronounce a number of words.
Teacher: "If a word ends with the same sound as you hear at the end of ten*t,* clap your hands once." For example: ves*t,* tub, ne*t,* Sally, co*t,* ki*te.*

2. Pairs of Words
Pronounce pairs of words, some of which end with the same sound. If the two words end with the same sound, the children respond *same;* if the final sounds are different, they say *different.*

For example:

net — but	*six — tax*	rub — rug
fan — fat	*bus — gas*	*lip — tap*
fog — pig	hat — hid	hop — hot
hen — man	leg — let	*log — bug*

(Start with C–V–C words and gradually include longer words.)

3. Using Pictures
Prepare a series of picture strips or duplicate a page consisting of lines containing four or five pictures. The pupil underlines each picture whose name ends with the same sound as the stimulus picture-word at the left.

Summary

The exercises in this chapter deal with teaching visual discrimination of letters and words and with noting speech sounds in words. These two skills are prerequisites for phonics instruction, which is defined as "teaching letter-sound relationships." Thus far, the child has not been asked to associate a given letter form with a specific speech sound. The next two chapters focus on teaching this skill.

5

Teaching Consonant Letter-Sound Relationships

We have so far dealt with skills that are prerequisites for learning letter-sound relationships. The two major ones are the ability to discriminate between letter forms and the ability to differentiate auditorily between speech sounds as heard in words. This chapter will focus on teachings that combine these skills and lead the child to associate a particular sound with a specific letter or combination of letters.

A Word about Sequence

The phonics program consists of many specific teachings. In any systematic program, this myriad of skills would have to be arranged into some teaching sequence. There are some options in regard to sequence that undoubtedly are of little educational consequence (such as whether to teach the sound of *t* before *b*, or *m* before *n*, etc.). On the other hand, the question of whether to teach consonant or vowel letter-sounds first is worthy of consideration.

Rationale for Teaching Consonant Sounds First

The majority of words children meet in beginning reading are words that begin with consonants. For instance, 175 (or approximately 80 percent) of the 220 words on the

Dolch Basic Sight Word Test begin with consonants. The Dale List of 769 Easy Words contains an even higher proportion (87%) of words beginning with consonants.

It is good learning theory to have the child start phonic analysis with the beginnings of words, working her way through the words from left to right. This reinforces the practice of reading from left to right and focuses the child's attention on the first part of the word. This is essential for facile reading and an absolute prerequisite if the child is to solve the word by sounding.

Consonants tend to be much more consistent than vowels in the sounds they represent. For instance, a number of consonants (*j, k, l, m, n, p, b, h, r, v, w*) represent only one sound. Certain other consonants that have two sounds present no problem in beginning reading instruction because one of the two basic sounds can be left until the child has had considerable practice in reading.

If a child uses skills in combination, sounding the initial consonant letter and using context-meaning clues will frequently be all the analysis that is needed. Assume each blank line in the following examples represents an unknown word:

1. _____ (This could represent *any* of 600,000 words in English.)
2. f_____ (Here, more than 98% of all words are eliminated. The unknown word *must* begin with the sound associated with the letter *f*.)

It is probable that the reader will arrive at the unknown word(s) in the following sentences despite the very limited context which is provided:

3. "You will have to pay the f_____ now," said the judge.
4. Without a doubt, pumpkin is my f_____ pie.
5. He took the stolen jewels to the f_____.
6. During J_____ it is much colder than it is in J_____ and J_____.

The sequence of teachings suggested in this chapter is:

1. Initial consonant letter-sounds
2. Initial consonant blends or clusters (*bl, st,* etc.)
3. Initial digraphs (*ch, wh, sh, th,* etc.)
4. Final consonants, blends, digraphs

Listing this sequence does not imply that all the possible steps under 1 must be completed before introducing any of the teachings in 2, 3, or 4. The procedures that follow illustrate some of the many approaches that can be used in teaching letter-sound relationships.

Consonants in Initial Position

One widely used technique for teaching initial letter-sounds is the use of children's names.

1. Write the names of several children in the class (or other common first names) that begin with the same letter (Bill, Betty, Ben, Bobby) on the chalkboard.
2. Pronounce each name; then have the class pronounce each name.
3. Call attention to the fact that each name begins with the same letter, and that this letter (B) represents the same sound in each word.

4. Use other series of names for other letter-sounds.

Jane	Denise	Mary	Sandy
Jerry	Dan	Matthew	Stan
Jill	Debra	Mike	Susan
John	Denny	Margaret	Sally

Other techniques for teaching initial letter-sounds follow.

Exercises: Initial Consonants

1. Chalkboard Drill
   For purposes of illustration, we will give the steps for teaching the sound of the consonant *m* in detail. All other consonant sounds can be taught in the same manner.
   a. Print the letter *m* (capital and lowercase) on the chalkboard. Indicate that for the next few minutes the group will study the sound of the letter *m* as it is heard in words. Write on the board a column of previously studied words, all of which begin with the letter *m*.
   b. Any words the children have met (as sight words) in experience charts or other materials may be used — words such as *me, must, moon, mind*. Also, familiar names of children in the class that call for capital letters may be used.

M	m
Mary	my
Mike	most
	man
	much
	milk

   c. Ask the children to look at the words carefully and name the letter that begins each word. Indicate that a big *M* or capital letter is used in names.
   d. As the teacher pronounces the words, the children are asked to listen to the sound heard at the beginning of each word. The initial sound is emphasized but not distorted.
   e. The children are then invited to read the words in unison, listening carefully to the sound of *m* as they say the words.
   f. Ask children to supply other words that begin with the sound of *m*.

2. Match a Pair
   This game is an adaptation of Concentration; it involves the use of pictures, and two or more children as participants (individual or team play).

Select pairs of pictures so that two picture-naming words begin with the same letter-sound: horse — hand; bell — boat; table — tub; fish — fox; desk — duck, etc. Shuffle the cards and lay them face down on the table.

The first player turns up two cards, hoping to match a pair of initial letter-sounds. If successful, he picks up both cards. If he does not match initial letter-sounds, both cards are again turned face down. Other players continue taking turns. (Each player attempts to note and remember the location of pictures that have been turned up but not matched.)

The winner is the player or team with the most pictures at the end of the game.

3. Building a Picture Dictionary

Use a supply of pictures from workbooks, magazines, and catalogues. Work with one letter at a time (B–b, for example).

After teaching the initial sound of B–b in words, have the children gather pictures whose naming words begin with that letter-sound. Children may work individually or in small groups.

Prepare a page (or several pages) for each letter-sound. Print a capital and lowercase letter at the top of the page and fill the page with pictures whose naming words begin with that letter-sound.

B–b

boot	bird	bed
bus	basket	book
barn	boat	boy

4. Print and Sound

Compile columns of easy words that begin with the letter-sounds to be taught or reviewed. Delete the initial letter, and provide space for the student to write the letter.

As she prints the initial letter, the child pronounces the word she has formed. (Material may be presented on the chalkboard, with transparencies, or as duplicated exercises.) Here are several examples.

a. Teacher: "In each blank space, add the letter above the column of words. Pronounce each word."

t	s	c	l
__ag	__ad	__ap	__og
__ub	__ix	__ot	__ap
__en	__un	__up	__ed
__op	__it	__an	__eg
__ip	__ob	__ub	__et

b. Teacher: "In each blank space, write one of the letters h, w, or g. Be sure the letter you choose makes a word. Pronounce the word."

__im	__ot	__ip	__ub
__et	__un	__ad	__id
__um	__ut	__ig	__ug
__eb	__en	__ap	__em

c. Teacher: "In each blank space, add any letter that will make a word."

__ug	__og	__eg	__at
__ox	__un	__it	__op
__ad	__ig	__ub	__in
__en	__an	__ot	__us

Mental Substitution

Day by day, in the early stages of reading instruction, the child is learning both sight words and the sounds of initial consonants. Knowledge thus gained can be applied in arriving at the pronunciation of other words not known as sight words. Assume the child knows the words *king* and *ring* and meets the unknown word *sing*. He should be able to combine the *s* sound, which he knows in words like *sat, some,* or *say,* with the sound of *ing* found in *king* and *ring*. This involves a process of "thinking the sounds." To illustrate, let us assume that:

1. A child has learned the italicized words in Table 5–1.
2. He has learned the sound of the initial consonant as heard in these italicized words.
3. He has not met or learned any of the other thirty-five words in Table 5–1.
4. By using his knowledge, plus some guidance from the teacher, he should be able to sound out all the words in Table 5–1.

TABLE 5–1 Sounding out words

bat	can	fit	had	map	pet	run	say
cat	ban	bit	bad	cap	bet	bun	bay
fat	fan	hit	fad	rap	met	fun	hay
hat	man	pit	mad	sap	set	sun	may
mat	pan	sit	pad				pay
pat	ran		sad				ray
rat							

By the process of thinking the sound of any known consonant and blending this sound with the phonogram that concludes a known sight word, the child should be able to pronounce the new word.

Exercises: Substitution

1. Place a known word on the board.
2. Have the children observe closely as you erase the initial *b* and substitute a different known consonant.

bat

___at

cat

3. Follow the same procedure, substituting other consonants to make easy words, such as *fat, hat, mat,* and *rat.*

For convenience in building mental substitution exercises, Table 5–2 provides a series of "word families." In each, the words end in a common phonogram (*et, ick, ack, ay, op, un, ill, am, ug, ed,* etc.). Not all the words in the table need to be used in beginning reading, and those beginning with blends should not be used in substitution exercises until the sounds of the blends have been taught.

1. Teacher: "Change the first letter and make a naming word for 'something living.' "

Example:
dish   ___ish   (*fish*)

log	___og	mitten	___itten
coat	___oat	rug	___ug
box	___ox	half	___alf
house	___ouse	nice	___ice
hat	___at	grow	___row
purse	___urse	pull	___ull

TABLE 5–2 Words for teaching substitution of initial consonant sounds (words with initial consonant blends are in parentheses)

back	bake	day	cap	bug	bank	cot	Dick
Jack	cake	hay	gap	dug	rank	dot	kick
lack	fake	lay	lap	hug	sank	got	lick
pack	lake	may	map	jug	tank	hot	nick
rack	make	pay	nap	mug	(blank)	lot	pick
sack	rake	ray	rap	rug	(crank)	not	sick
tack	sake	say	tap	tug	(drank)	pot	(brick)
(black)	take	way	(clap)	(drug)	(flank)	(blot)	(click)
(crack)	wake	(clay)	(flap)	(plug)	(frank)	(plot)	(slick)
(slack)	(brake)	(play)	(slap)	(slug)	(plank)	(shot)	(stick)
(stack)	(flake)	(stray)	(snap)	(smug)	(prank)	(spot)	(thick)
(track)	(snake)	(tray)	(trap)	(snug)	(spank)	(trot)	(trick)
bag	bail	gain	bat	bump	can	came	Bill
gag	fail	lain	cat	dump	Dan	dame	fill
lag	hail	main	fat	hump	fan	fame	hill
nag	mail	pain	hat	jump	man	game	kill
rag	nail	rain	mat	lump	pan	lame	mill
sag	pail	vain	pat	pump	ran	name	pill
tag	rail	(brain)	rat	(plump)	tan	same	will
wag	sail	(drain)	sat	(slump)	van	tame	(drill)
(brag)	tail	(grain)	(brat)	(stump)	(bran)	(blame)	(skill)
(drag)	(frail)	(plain)	(flat)	(trump)	(clan)	(flame)	(spill)
(flag)	(trail)	(train)	(scat)		(plan)	(frame)	(still)
(snag)	(snail)						
best	bet	bunk	bell	bit	dim	dear	bad
lest	get	dunk	fell	fit	him	fear	dad
nest	jet	hunk	sell	hit	Jim	hear	fad
pest	let	junk	tell	pit	rim	near	had
rest	met	sunk	well	sit	Tim	rear	lad
test	net	(drunk)	yell	wit	(brim)	tear	mad
vest	pet	(flunk)	(smell)	(flit)	(grim)	year	pad
zest	set	(skunk)	(spell)	(grit)	(slim)	(clear)	sad
(blest)	wet	(spunk)	(swell)	(slit)	(swim)	(smear)	(glad)
(crest)	(fret)	(trunk)		(split)	(trim)	(spear)	

2. Teacher: "On the line following each word, write a new word by changing the first letter to the next letter in the alphabet. Then pronounce the new word."

bake	_____	cot	_____	fun	_____
ball	_____	cry	_____	fame	_____
book	_____	candy	_____	fate	_____
but	_____	crop	_____	fold	_____
gold	_____	lad	_____	met	_____
got	_____	lake	_____	moon	_____
gate	_____	let	_____	mine	_____
gum	_____	line	_____	meat	_____
		lap	_____	mice	_____

Difficulty level can be increased by mixing the words instead of presenting a series of four words.

boat	_____	map	_____	sail	_____
cash	_____	run	_____	rat	_____
fang	_____	sight	_____	bold	_____
gay	_____	bat	_____	sack	_____
kit	_____	kick	_____	ring	_____
lay	_____	vest	_____	kid	_____

Context Plus Minimal Phonic Cue

This exercise illustrates that, in many situations, the context plus the phonic cue provided by the initial letter of an unknown word will provide enough clues to solve the unknown word. The blank space in each sentence under A could be replaced with several different words. The same blank space in sentences under B provide the initial consonant letter of the word. Have children note that when they heed this phonic cue, they can eliminate many of the previously acceptable choices.

Directions: Read sentences under A. Have children provide a number of words that could fit in each blank. Then read sentences under B and have them note their general agreement on choices.

A. 1. The _____ would not start.
   2. "She is my _____," said Billy.
   3. Billy asked, "How much _____ do we have?"
   4. Which _____ of the year is your favorite?
   5. What word _____ in the blank space?
B. 1. The c_____ would not start.
   2. "She is my s_____," said Billy.

3. Billy asked, "How much m_____ do we have?"
4. Which t_____ of the year is your favorite?
5. What word f_____ in the blank space?

Oral exercise
Directions: Have a volunteer read one of the incomplete sentences, adding any word that will logically conclude the sentence. Other students then volunteer other words that fit. Stress that no word can fit unless it begins with the sound represented by the letter shown.

Written exercise
Children write one (or more) words that begin with the letter shown.

1. Can you see the p_____?
2. Is this your b_____?
3. This is a t_____.
4. Here is the d_____.
5. The girls felt very s_____.

Context Clues and Phonic Skills: Working Together

Under less than optimal teaching practices, phonics instruction can be so far removed from *reading* that it inhibits learning to read. All phonics instruction, however, need not focus exclusively on letter-sound relationships. Reading instruction can be made more effective if the learning task involves both reading (context) and a phonics task whose completion depends on the reading task.

In this chapter, as well as in following chapters, phonics instruction is imbedded in a "Fun with Language" approach. The learner is asked to read in order to discover what phonics task he is being asked to perform. The difficulty levels of these exercises range from one word clues, to phrases, and sentences. These materials can be adapted to almost any phonic teaching: initial, medial, final consonants; blends, digraphs, vowel patterns, etc. In all of these exercises, the teacher reads the directions and any sample items with the student.

Exercises: Using Context

Teacher: "Read the clue. What do they do? Write the correct word in the space."

Clue			Clue		
dogs	_____	(bark, dark)	cows	_____	(moo, boo)
birds	_____	(sly, fly)	bells	_____	(wing, ring)
boats	_____	(hail, sail)	fires	_____	(turn, burn)
horses	_____	(run, fun)	kings	_____	(mule, rule)
towels	_____	(cry, dry)	frogs	_____	(hop, mop)

Teacher: "Read the clue. Complete the word that fits the clue. Use one of the letters *c* or *t* to make a word that fits the clue."

Example:

| pretty | __ute | use c to spell *cute* |
| story | __ale | use t to spell *tale* |

	Clue			Clue	
1.	money	__ash	6.	speaking	__alk
2.	bath	__ub	7.	knives	__ut
3.	brush	__eeth	8.	Christmas	__ard
4.	bird	__age	9.	gentle	__ame
5.	spins	__op	10.	penny	__ent

Teacher: "Write one of the letters *p* or *n* in each blank space to make a word that fits the clue."

1.	fruit	__ear	6.	loud	__oise
2.	bird	__est	7.	medicine	__ill
3.	fence	__ost	8.	pecan kernel	__ut
4.	two	__air	9.	sharp	__eedle
5.	close	__ear	10.	writes	__en

Teacher: "Read the clue. Add the first letter to make a word that fits the clue."

Example:
You can read it: __ook (b)

	Clue		Clue
1.	not small: __ig	6.	season before winter: __all
2.	lives on farm: __ig	7.	not short: __all
3.	false hair: __ig	8.	round and bounces: __all
4.	a dance step: __ig	9.	from floor to ceiling: __all
5.	make a hole in the ground: __ig	10.	shopping center: __all

Teacher: "Write the letter that spells the word that fits the clue. Use *p, b,* or *d.*"

	Clue			Clue	
1.	we read it	__ook	6.	goes around waist	__elt
2.	please open the	__oor	7.	we sleep on it	__ed
3.	lives on a farm	__ig	8.	worth 10 cents	__ime
4.	goes on the water	__oat	9.	place where we play	__ark
5.	a dog is a	__et	10.	at night it is	__ark

Teacher: "Change the first letter in each *underlined* word so that the new word names something living."

Examples:
I can change <u>big</u> to __ig. (*pig*)
I can change <u>see</u> to __ee. (*bee*)

I can change:
hat to __at
dish to __ish
pen to __en
toy to __oy

If a child or group has difficulty with a particular consonant letter sound, develop exercises which focus on this letter. (The exercise which follows illustrates *c* and *f*.)

Teacher: "Read the clue. Write the letter that spells the word that fits the clue."

Set 1			Set 2		
1.	wear on head	__ap	1.	not slow	__ast
2.	catches mice	__at	2.	lives in water	__ish
3.	not hot	__old	3.	more than four	__ive
4.	grows on farm	__orn	4.	after summer	__all
5.	baby cow	__alf	5.	less than five	__our
6.	ice cream	__one	6.	good to eat	__ood
7.	a baby bear	__ub	7.	a tree	__ir

Fun with Language

1. Teacher: "Read the clues (be careful, they're tricky). Complete the word that fits the clue. Use one of the consonant letters *d, f, s,* or *g* to spell the word that fits the clue."

Example:

Clue		
not much money	__ime	*D* is the only letter that makes a word; a dime is not much money.
front of head	__ace	Choose *F*, makes sense.
four legs and butts	__oat	*G* spells goat, which has four legs. Have you ever heard of a goat butting someone?

Clue			Clue		
1.	not back, not front	__ide	6.	don't _____ the bears	__eed
2.	1492 . . . 1776 . . . 1976	__ates	7.	always number one	__irst
3.	hole in one	__olf	8.	not here now	__one
4.	damp minus p	__am	9.	what I owe you	__ebt
5.	goes in shoes	__eet	10.	like the others	__ame

2. The 3–C Sentences!
   In the sentences below:

   A. Candy is a girl's name. (Candy starts with a capital letter!)
   B. She has a candy cane.
   C. The three c's get all mixed up, but when you read for meaning it's easy.

Teacher: "Fill in each blank space with one of these words — Candy, candy, or cane."
Problem: _____ has a _____ _____.
Solved: Candy has a candy cane.

1. Does _____ have a _____ _____?
2. Yes, the _____ _____ belongs to _____.
3. Will _____ eat her _____ _____?
4. _____ may eat the _____ _____.
5. Then _____ will not have a _____ _____.
6. This ends the story of _____ and her _____
   _____.

3. B(ware) — B(ready) — B(sharp)
   Teacher: "Every blank space in the following sentences can be filled with the following 'B words' — book, boy, bus. As you read each sentence write the correct word in each blank space."

   1. The _____ has a _____.
   2. The _____ took the _____ on a _____.
   3. The _____ left the _____ on the _____.
   4. The _____ driver found the _____.
   5. He gave the _____ to the _____.
   6. Now the _____ has the _____.
   7. Will the _____ read the _____?
   8. The _____ read the _____, but not on the
      _____!

4. Double D Words
   Teacher: "The word *dog* will fit in one space in each sentence below. *One other word* that also begins with *d* will fit in each of the other spaces. Complete the sentences."

   1. _____ the _____ with the towel.
   2. The towel will _____ the _____.
   3. The _____ can _____ off in the sun.
   4. Will the sun _____ the _____?
   5. Keep the _____ _____ in winter.

5. More Double D Words
   Teacher: "The word *dog* will fit in one blank space in each sentence below. Fill the other space with a word that begins with *d*."

   Example:
   _____ said, "Where is the _____?"
      (Dad)   said, "Where is the (dog) ?"

   1. The d_____ sat by the d_____.
   2. The artist said, "I will d_____ a d_____.
   3. The d_____ will d_____ the water.
   4. D_____ the d_____ d_____ a hole in the
      yard?

5. Yes, the d_____ d_____ d_____ a hole in the yard!

"Need a little help? These words fit the spaces: dog, did, dig, drink, draw, door."

6. Fun with Triple D Words

Teacher: "Each sentence has *three* missing words. Each missing word begins with the letter *d*. The words *dig, did,* and *dad* fit in each sentence. Where does each word fit?"

Example:

D _____ d_____ d_____ this hole?
(Did)   (dad)   (dig)   this hole?

1. D_____ said he d_____ d_____ that hole.
2. D_____ d_____ d_____ the hole.
3. When d_____ d_____ d_____ that hole?
4. D_____ d_____ not d_____ the hole today.

Teaching Consonant Blends

Consonant blends consist of two or more letters that are blended when pronouncing the word. If a child attempts to sound separately each of the consonants in a blend, distortion and confusion will result. These sounds must be blended to arrive at the correct pronunciation. The child *knows these speech sounds*—she must learn to recognize their printed equivalents. For example, the pupil knows the sound of *s*, as heard in *see, sit, some, say,* and the sound of *t*, as heard in *tell, to, talk, top*. The next short step, from the known to the unknown, would be teaching the blend sound *st*, as heard in *stop, still, stand,* and the like.

Two- and three-letter consonant blends may be divided into three major groups on the basis of a common letter:

- Those in which *r* is the concluding letter (Column A)
- Those in which *l* is the concluding letter (Column B)
- Those which begin with the letter *s* (Column C)

A		B		C
br	scr	bl	spl	sc
cr	spr	cl		sk
dr	str	fl		sm
fr	thr	gl		sn
gr		pl		sp
pr		sl		st
tr				sw

The blends are listed alphabetically, but may be taught in any order. The two-letter blends are easier to learn and occur more frequently in words met in beginning reading than do the three-letter blends; therefore, it is better to teach the two-letter blends first. See Table 5–3 (p. 69) for words which can be used in teaching consonant blends.

There are several ways to teach children how to master these blend sounds. Regardless of what approach you use, the objectives in teaching blends are to have the child: (a) see the letter combination involved; (b) realize that in every case the letters combine into a blend sound; and (c) discriminate between the blend sound and the sound of individual letters, for example, *pay, lay, play.*

Procedures for teaching initial blends closely parallel those for teaching initial consonant sounds. To illustrate, we will look at the steps in teaching the sound represented by *st* in detail. All other consonant blends may be taught in the same manner.

Chalkboard Drill

Place a few *st* words on the board, such as stop, still, star, stand, stick. Direct children's attention to the *st* beginning. As each word is pronounced, ask pupils to listen to the *st* sound in initial position. Then invite the children to give other words that begin with the blended sounds *st* (stone, star, stood, stir, etc.).

Auditory-Visual Association

1. Key words (two-letter blends)
   a. Duplicate a series of key words that emphasize the common letter in a number of consonant blends (such as *r, l, s*). Provide each child with a copy.
   b. Lead children in seeing and saying the blends and the key words in each column: *br* as in *bring; cr* as in *cry; dr* as in *drum,* etc.

See the r		See the l		Begins with s	
br	bring	bl	blue	sc	school
cr	cry	cl	clean	sk	sky
dr	drum	fl	fly	sm	small
fr	from	gl	glad	sn	snow
gr	green	pl	play	sp	spot
pr	pretty	sl	slow	st	stop
tr	tree			sw	swim

2. Hearing blends in words (identifying blends heard)
   a. Prepare columns showing three different blends.
   b. Pronounce a word that begins with one of the blends shown: "blue," "stand," "train," and so on.
   c. Children underline the blend that is heard at the beginning of the stimulus word.

blue	stand	train	play	smoke
br	st	gl	pr	sn
pl	sl	tr	bl	sm
bl	sm	sk	pl	sp

3. Word recognition (auditory-to-visual patterns)
   a. Duplicate a number of three-word series as shown below.
   b. Pronounce one word from each series. (The stimulus word is *italicized* here, but would not be on hand-out material supplied to children.)
   c. Children underline the word pronounced.

	1	2	3	4	5
	black	stay	smell	skin	*flew*
	back	gay	*spell*	*sing*	few
	brick	*gray*	sell	swing	true
	6	7	8	9	10
	snail	sin	dumb	grain	bake
	scale	sink	*drum*	rain	*brake*
	sail	*skin*	from	gain	rake

Exercises: Print and Sound

1. Add a Blend
   Here the pupil writes the two letters that represent the initial blended sounds.
   Teacher: "Write the letters that are shown above the blank spaces. Then pronounce the words you have made."

br	sp	cl	sw
_____ain	_____eak	_____ean	_____im
_____ake	_____oon	_____oth	_____eet
_____an	_____ace	_____ay	_____an
_____own	_____in	_____imb	_____ell
_____ush	_____ell	_____ock	_____ing

2. Change a Blend
   Use word endings that will make different words when different blends are added.
   Teacher: "In each blank space write the blend shown on the left. Then pronounce each word."

(br) _____own	(sp) _____ill	(sk) _____ate
(cr) _____own	(st) _____ill	(pl) _____ate
(dr) _____own	(sk) _____ill	(st) _____ate
(fr) _____own	(dr) _____ill	(cr) _____ate
	(gr) _____ill	(sl) _____ate

Exercises: Using Context

Teacher: "Read the clue. Write a two letter blend to make a word that goes with the clue."

Examples:

snake _____awls
(a snake *crawls*—so use *cr*)
fruit _____and
(you can buy fruit at the fruit *stand*)
(Note: All tasks in Set 1 begin with the same blend found in the clue. In Set 2 they are all different.)

Set 1		Set 2	
Clue		*Clue*	
fresh	_____uit	snow	_____ake
tree	_____unk	broom	_____eeps
train	_____ack	scare	_____ow
brown	_____ead	draw	_____idge
sleds	_____ide	glue	_____icks
travel	_____ip	free	_____ess

Teacher: "Read the clue. Complete the word that fits the clue. Use one of the blends *st, sp,* or *sn* to make a word that fits the clue."

Examples:

a place to buy:	_____ore	use *st* to spell *store*
football, tennis:	_____orts	use *sp* to spell *sports*

Clue		*Clue*	
1. hard metal:	_____eel	6. to say something:	_____eak
2. slow as a:	_____ail	7. shines at night:	_____ar
3. tops do this:	_____in	8. sleep noise:	_____ore
4. eat with this:	_____oon	9. bees can:	_____ing
5. to begin:	_____art	10. as white as:	_____ow

Teacher: "Write one of the blends *sl, sw,* or *sk* in the blank spaces to make a word that fits the clue."

Clue		*Clue*	
1. using a broom:	_____eep	6. above the earth:	_____y
2. women wear:	_____irts	7. moves on snow:	_____ed
3. not fast:	_____ow	8. a beautiful fowl:	_____an
4. very clever:	_____y	9. arm goes in:	_____eeve
5. a bunch of bees:	_____arm	10. smells bad:	_____unk

Teacher: "Write the blend that spells the word that fits the clue."

Examples:
pleased and happy _____ad (gl)
train runs on it _____ack (tr)

Clue Box				
sl	tr	bl	cl	sp

1. near by   _____ose
2. close your eyes and   _____eep
3. what a top does   _____in
4. cannot see   _____ind
5. used to catch lobsters   _____ap

6. to go up the hill   _____imb
7. train runs on it   _____ack
8. to say something   _____eak
9. a pretty color   _____ue
10. not very fast   _____ow

Teacher: "Read the clue. Write the word that fits the clue."

Example:
can write on this: _____ (skate, *slate*)

         Clue
1. food is placed on this: _____   (state, plate)
2. not big or large: _____   (small, star)
3. this jumps in the pond: _____   (frog, drop)
4. not very far away: _____   (slow, close)
5. what we do with a broom: _____   (sweep, speak)

Teacher: "How many *students* can *stand* on a *stump*? Each of these sentences has two missing words. The words *stand* and *stump* will fit in each sentence. Where does each word fit?"

Examples:
Can you _____ on a _____?
This is easy; the context forces you to write:
Can you *stand* on a *stump?*
Finish the following sentences.

1. You can _____ on a _____.
2. A _____ can _____ in the woods.
3. A _____ can _____ a long time.
4. We can both _____ on this large _____.
5. Can this _____ _____ for fifty years?

Teacher: "Since you are well *grounded* in reading, it will be easy to *plow* through this exercise. Just *plant* a few words in the blank spaces. Each sentence has two missing words. Two of the words, *plow, plant,* or *ground,* will fit in each sentence. Which two words fit where?"

Examples:
After you _____ you can _____ crops.
When you use the context of the sentence, you will probably make it read:
After you *plow* you can *plant* crops.

Complete each of the following sentences using *plow*, *plant* or *ground*.

1. You must _____ the _____ in the spring.
2. Then you _____ seeds in the _____.
3. You must _____ before you _____.
4. Remember, _____ seed after you _____.
5. Always prepare the _____ before you _____.

Teacher: "One of the letter clusters in the clue box will complete *all* the words in *one* sentence. Study each sentence and fill in the blanks."

Clue Box				
gr	cl	tr	st	dr

Example:
They _____ew many kinds of _____ain on the farm. (gr)

1. The _____own will _____ean the _____othes.
2. He _____ood ready to _____art telling the _____ory.
3. She did not _____op the _____um during the _____ill.
4. It was a _____eat to _____amp along the _____ail.
5. She _____ove to town to buy a _____ess.

Teacher: "John makes many speeches. The sentences which follow are all about John and his speeches. All blanks in these sentences are filled by one of these words:

  speak   spoke   spoken   speaking   speaks   speaker

(Wait—The last word in the last sentence begins with a different blend.)"

1. John was invited to sp_____.
2. He is sp_____ now.
3. He will sp_____ again tomorrow.
4. He sp_____ twice this week.
5. He has sp_____ many times this year.
6. He is a very good sp_____.
7. After he sp_____ he will eat a _____eak!!

Teaching Consonant Digraphs (*sh, wh, th, ch*)

Digraphs are combinations of two letters that represent one speech sound. The sound heard is not a blend of the two letters involved, but a completely new sound. A given digraph may have more than one pronunciation, but the letter combination results in a single sound in each case (*ch* = *k* in "chorus"; *sh* in "chef"; *ch* in "church"). Digraphs may be taught in a similar way to that used for teaching consonant sounds.

TABLE 5–3 Words for teaching initial consonant blends

br	cr	dr	fr	gr	pr	tr
brother	cry	dress	friend	grade	pretty	tree
bring	cross	drink	from	great	present	train
brought	crop	draw	front	ground	president	trip
brown	creek	dry	Friday	green	program	truly
brake	crowd	drive	fruit	grandmother	print	trick
bread	cream	drop	fright	grass	produce	truck
bright	crack	dream	free	grandfather	prize	trade
bridge	crawl	drove	fresh	group	promise	trap
break	crib	drum	frog	grew	proud	track
brave	cried	drew	freeze	gray	product	true
brush	crumb	drill	frozen	grain	prepare	trail
branch	crown	drag	friendly	grab	protect	treat
brick	crow	drank	fry	grape	press	trim
broom	crook	drug	frost	grand	price	tramp

bl	cl	fl	pl	sl	sp	st
black	close	flower	play	sleep	spell	start
blue	clean	fly	place	sled	spend	stay
blow	class	floor	please	slid	spot	story
block	clothes	flag	plant	slate	speak	stop
bloom	climb	flew	plan	slip	spent	store
blew	club	flood	plane	slowly	sport	study
blanket	cloth	float	plenty	slave	speed	still
blood	cloud	flat	plain	slow	spoke	state
blackboard	clear	flour	plate	slipper	spirit	stand
blossom	clay		pleasant	slept	speech	stick
blind	clothing	gl	plow	sleet	spoon	stocking
blame	clock	glad	player	sleepy	spear	step
blizzard	climate	glass	plantation	slim	space	star
blaze	clown	glove	playmate	slick	spin	stood

sc	sk	sm	sn	sw	tw	
school	skate	small	snow	swim	twelve	
scare	skin	smoke	snake	sweet	twist	
scold	sky	smell	snowball	swing	twenty	
scout	ski	smile	snail	sweater	twice	
scream	skip	smart	snap	swan	twin	
schoolhouse	skirt	smooth	snug	sweep	twig	
score	skunk	smack	sneeze	swell	twinkle	

Steps in Brief

1. Place several stimulus words on the chalkboard: *shall, she, ship, show.*
2. Ask the children to look at the words carefully and note how they are alike. Draw out the observation that all words begin with *sh.* (Underline the digraph being taught: *sh, ch, th, wh.*)
3. Ask the children to listen to the sound of *sh* as they say the words together.
4. Invite children to supply other words that begin with the same sound as "shall," "she," "ship," "show."

Note: The digraph *sh* usually has the sound heard in these stimulus words. Other common *sh* words are: *shut, shop, shot, sheep, shape, shade, short, sheet, shoot, shoe, shell, shirt, shovel, shake, sharp, shine.*

The digraph *wh* is usually pronounced as if spelled *hw*: when = hwen; white = hwite. The *wh* sound may be taught as is *sh* above, with *when, white, what,* and *which* as stimulus words. Other common *wh* words are: *why, where, wheel, wheat, whisper, whether, whale, whiskers.* Exceptions: When *o* follows *wh,* the *w* is silent; who = hōō; whole = hōl; whom = hōōm; whose = hōōz. (Changing patterns of pronunciation will likely find some dictionaries recognizing a second pronunciation: When = wĕn.)

The digraph *th* has two common sounds. There is the voiced *th* sound as in *this, their, they, though, that, then, there, than,* and *them,* and the unvoiced *th* sound as in *thing, thin, thimble, thank, think, thick, third,* and *thumb.* (The concepts of *voiced* and *unvoiced* need not be taught in relation to reading.)

While the consonant digraph *ch* has three different sounds, the most common and the one met almost exclusively in beginning reading is that of *ch* heard in *chair* or *chop.*

Common words for use in teaching exercises are:

chair	chin	chose	charm	chalk
child	check	chop	chance	cheer
chicken	cheek	change	chimney	chief

Much later, children will meet the other sounds represented by *ch.* (These need not be taught in beginning reading.)

ch = k		*ch = sh*	
chorus	(kō rus)	chef	(shef)
character	(kar ak ter)	chassis	(shas ē)
chemist	(kem ist)	chauffeur	(sho fur)
choir	(kwir)	chic	(shēk)
chord	(kord)	chiffon	(shif on)
chrome	(krom)	chamois	(sham ē)

Sentence Drill

Prepare a number of sentences in which a high percentage of the words begin with the digraphs *sh, ch, wh, th.* These may be presented via the chalkboard, transparencies, or duplicated worksheets. After reading the material silently, children volunteer to read a sentence to the group.

1. Charles and Chip chatted in the church chapel.
2. Chester chose a chunk of cheese and some chips from the chest.
3. Shirley showed the shells to Sherman.
4. The shepherd sheltered the sheep in the shadow of the shed.
5. His white whiskers were whirled by the whistling wind.
6. Mr. White whispered when and where the whale would appear.
7. On Thursday, Thelma thought of thirty things to do.
8. Thad thought about a thorn in his thumb.

Exercises: Using Context

Teacher: "Read the clue word. Following each clue, complete a word that has the opposite meaning. Use one of the digraphs ch, th, sh, wh to do this."

Example:
Clue
pride: _____ame (write *sh* for shame)

	Clue			Clue	
1.	adult:	_____ild	6.	dull:	_____arp
2.	tall:	_____ort	7.	retreat:	_____arge
3.	open:	_____ut	8.	freeze:	_____aw
4.	fat:	_____in	9.	thin:	_____ick
5.	shout:	_____isper	10.	warm:	_____illy

Teacher: "Read the clue. Build a word (use *ch, sh, th, wh*) that fits the clue."

Example:
can dig with this: _____ovel (sh)

	Clue	
1.	fits on foot:	_____oe
2.	not very tall:	_____ort
3.	round and rolls:	_____eel
4.	speaking very softly:	_____isper
5.	writes on blackboard:	_____alk
6.	leader of the tribe:	_____ief
7.	one on each hand:	_____umb
8.	after first and second:	_____ird
9.	we sit on this:	_____air
10.	found on the beach:	_____ell

Teacher: "Each sentence shows two words containing blank spaces. One digraph (*ch, sh, th, wh*) will fit the blanks in both words. Study each sentence and complete each word."

Example:
Don't let the (*ch*)icken eat the (*ch*)alk.

1. The _____eep were resting in the _____ade.
2. Who put the _____alk mark on the _____air?
3. _____ich of the _____eels is broken?
4. He bought a _____irt in the _____op.
5. She had a _____imble on her _____umb.
6. After a purchase, always _____eck your _____ange.

Fun With Language

Teacher: "Each sentence below contains some incomplete words. A digraph *ch–th–sh–wh* is missing in each word. Read the clue box carefully and then complete the sentences."

```
┌─────────────────────────────────────────────┐
│                  Clue Box                     │
│  Chuck and Sue plan to go shopping.           │
│  Knowing this will help you.                  │
│  Remember the missing parts are ch–th–sh–wh.  │
└─────────────────────────────────────────────┘
```

1. Sue said, "_____ere _____all we _____op?"
2. _____uck said, "And _____at _____all we buy?"
3. I _____ink we _____ould _____eck the ads," said _____uck.
4. _____en I will _____op for _____oes and a _____irt.
5. Sue wanted to _____op for _____ite _____oes.
6. I _____ink _____ey _____ould have fun _____ile _____opping!

The wh Roundup

(Tease out the meaning)
In the following sentences:
Each unfinished word begins with *wh*.
*Wh*ich word goes *where*?
Clue: All sentences are based on the clue box.

```
┌─────────────────────────────────────────────┐
│                  Clue Box                     │
│  "Sam lives in a white house on Whale Street."│
└─────────────────────────────────────────────┘
```

Finish each word so that it makes sense in the sentence.

1. Wh_____ house on Wh_____ Street is Sam's house?
2. Sam lives on Wh_____ Street in a wh_____ house.

3. Sam, wh_____ house is wh_____, lives on
   Wh_____ Street.

4. Wh_____ house is the wh_____ house
   wh_____ Sam lives?

5. Wh_____ on Wh_____ Street is Sam's
   wh_____ house?

6. Wh_____ did Sam move into the wh_____ house?

Consonant Sounds at Ends of Words

Some of the procedures for teaching initial sounds can be adapted to teaching final sounds. The teaching objective remains the same — to help children visually recognize letter forms and associate these with the sounds they represent in words.

Exercises

1. Chalkboard Drill
   a. Select letter-sound to be taught.
   b. Place stimulus words on board.
   c. Call children's attention to final letter.
   d. Pronounce each word carefully, so that children hear the sound at the end of the word.
   e. Have children pronounce words and supply others that end with the sound.

2. Print and Sound
   a. Prepare columns of easy words, all of which end with a particular letter-sound.
   b. Omit the final letter.
   c. The child prints the letter indicated and pronounces the word.

Add *d*	Add *n*	Add *p*	Add *g*	Add *t*
sa__	gu__	li__	ho__	ne__
mu__	wi__	ca__	pi__	hu__
ha__	te__	na__	ta__	co__
ro__	ru__	cu__	wi__	hi__

Variation:
Add one of the letters *m–x–b* to make a word.
Pronounce each word.

bo__	gu__	ro__	dru__	fo__
roo__	mi__	ha__	gra__	so__
hi__	tu__	si__	wa__	ta__

Change the last letter of words in the first column so that the new word names something living.

Example:
pin → pi__ (g) pig
plane → plan__ (t) plant

1. but	bu_____	6. map	ma_____
2. lamp	lam_____	7. dot	do_____
3. fog	fo_____	8. hem	he_____
4. call	cal_____	9. owe	ow_____
5. cap	ca_____	10. sharp	shar_____

Exercise: Using Context

Teacher: "Finish each sentence below so that it 'makes sense'. Put the letter *m* or *n* in each blank space. You must read carefully to know which letter fits into which blank."

Example:
Pa__ had a talk with a ma__.
No sense→ Pan had a talk with a mam.
Correct→ Pam had a talk with a man.
Remember that every blank has to be filled with *m* or *n*.

1. Sa__ can count to te__.
2. Ca__ you see the me__?
3. She gave hi__ a stick of gu__.
4. Please pass the ha__.
5. Mo__ put ja__ on the bu__.

Purpose: To provide practice in hearing the letter sounds *p–d–b* at the end of words.
Teacher: "Finish each sentence below so that it makes sense. Put one of the letters *b–d–p* in each blank space. You must read carefully to know which letter fits in each space."

Example:
A baby bear is a cu___. (can't be cup or cud)
A baby bear is a cub.

Set 1

1. Turn on the lam___.
2. They rode in a taxi ca___.
3. A baby sheep is a lam___.
4. He took a short na___.
5. I like corn on a co___.
6. A bee stung him on the han___.

Set 2

Put one of the letters *b–d–p* in each blank space.

1. Bo___ plays in the ban___.
2. The guide said, "Here is the ma___."
3. The water in the tu___ was col___.
4. Di___ he leave his ca___ in the ca___?
5. Mother said, "Gra___ the pu___."

These are some stimulus words to use in board or seatwork exercises:

b	*d*	*f*	*g*	*k(ck)*	*l(ll)*	*m*
Bob	sad	if	dog	back	call	him
tub	fed	calf	big	rock	tell	room
club	send	muff	flag	black	hill	gum
grab	glad	stiff	rug	trick	pull	ham
rob	cold	puff	drug	duck	still	whom
rib	band	off	bag	pick	small	drum

n	*p*	*r*	*s(s)*	*s(=z)*	*t*
can	hop	for	bus	his	cat
win	cap	star	yes	as	met
men	stop	her	dress	ours	shut
thin	up	dear	us	is	hit
when	step	door	less	has	set
ran	skip	clear	likes	runs	sat
moon	map	car	miss	days	but

Consonant Digraphs (*ch, sh, th*) at Ends of Words

The *sounds* of the digraphs *ch*, *sh*, and *th* will have been taught as they occur at the beginning of words. Procedures for teaching these sounds at the end of words may parallel those used for teaching initial sounds.

1. Place stimulus words on board.
2. Have children "see" the letter combinations under discussion.
3. Pronounce each word carefully so children *hear* the sound at the end of the word.
4. Have children pronounce words.
5. Other stimulus words ending with *ch—sh—th* are *March, church, peach, branch, ditch, search, teach, patch, bench; fish, cash, fresh, rush, crash, dish, flash, wish, push; both, bath, tenth, north, health, path, length, fifth, cloth.*

```
Which
reach
such
pitch
```

Exercises: Using Context

Teacher: "Read the clue word. Complete the word that follows, using one of the digraphs *ch–th–sh*.

Clue word		Clue word	
fruit:	pea_____	vegetable:	squa_____
two:	bo_____	direction:	nor_____
month:	Mar_____	meal:	lun_____
money:	ca_____	insect:	mo_____
lightning:	fla_____	wreck:	cra_____
trail:	pa_____	worship:	chur_____

Teacher: "Some language games are easier than they look!
To complete the following sentences you must write one of the digraphs *ch–sh–th* in each blank space. Reading the rest of the sentence makes it easy."

Example:
Eat fre_____ fi_____ for your heal_____.
The only way for the sentence to make sense is by using *sh–sh–th* in the three blanks.
Remember: Either *ch, sh,* or *th* will fit in each blank.

1. "Are the fi_____ fre_____?," he asked.
2. Bo_____ nor_____ and sou_____ are directions.
3. A bran_____ fell from the pea_____ tree.
4. The parade will mar_____ down the pa_____.
5. Whi_____ clo_____ needs the pat_____?
6. We had fre_____ fi_____ for lun_____.
7. Mar_____ is the third mon_____.

Consonant Digraphs (*nk, ng, ck*) at the Ends of Words

Teaching *nk, ng,* and *ck* involves associating these letter combinations at the end of words or syllables with the sounds they represent. These digraphs may be taught as follows; for example, "The sound of *nk* at the end of words is the sound we hear in these words."

bank	link	junk
rank	mink	sunk
sank	pink	drunk
tank	sink	shrunk

Other words to use in board or seatwork exercises include: *ink, blink, drink, think; plank, drank, spank, frank; trunk, chunk, bunk.*

"The sound of *ng* at the end of words is the sound we hear in these words."

bang	king	gong	hung
gang	ring	bong	rung
hang	wing	strong	sprung
sang	sing	song	sung

"The letters *ck* have the sound of *k*. Listen to the sound at the end of these words."

back	pick	dock	luck
pack	kick	lock	duck
sack	sick	block	truck
crack	trick	sock	buck

Final Consonant Blends (*st, sk, ld, mp, nd*)

Teaching procedures described throughout this chapter can be used or adapted to teach blended consonants occurring at the end of words (*st, sk, ld, mp, nd*):

must	ask	cold	jump	find
fast	desk	wild	camp	band
rest	mask	field	dump	found
most	dusk	child	champ	bend

Consonant Irregularities

Fortunately, sounds represented by consonant letters involve less variability than is found in vowel letter-sounds. Nevertheless, a number of consonants and consonant combinations result in pronunciation irregularities that must be taught. The majority of these fall under one of the following headings:

- Consonants that have more than one sound (for example, c sounded as k or s; g sounded as g or j; and s sounded as s–z = sh or zh).
- Consonants that are not sounded (know, light, wrap)
- Consonant combinations with unique pronunciations (ph = f; que = k)

Teaching the Two Sounds of C (k and s)

The letter c represents no distinctive sound of its own. It is sounded as k when followed by the vowels a, o, and u and as s when followed by i, e, or y. The hard (k) sound occurs most frequently and for this reason is usually taught first. Eight words on the Dolch List begin with the letter c, and in all of these the letter has its k sound. Only four of the fifty-eight words on the Dale List that begin with c have the s sound. Chalkboard and duplicated seat-work exercises can provide drill as needed. Here are some examples.

c is sounded k when followed by:	a	o	u
	call	cold	cut
	cake	come	cup
	care	coat	cute
	cap	cook	cub
c is sounded s when followed by:	i	e	y
	city	cent	cycle
	cider	cement	cypress
	circle	mice	bicycle
	citizen	voice	cyclone

Exercise: Sounds of C

Teacher: "On each blank space write s or k to show the sound of the letter c."

_____ cat   _____ comb   _____ ceiling   _____ color

_____ center   _____ citizen   _____ cuff   _____ cellar

Teaching the Two Sounds of G (g and j)

1. The letter g has its regular (hard) sound when followed by a, u, and o.
2. The letter g is often sounded as j when followed by i, e, and y. (Common exceptions: give, girl, get, geese, gift.)

Dealing with the two sounds of g is not so much a matter of "teaching" but of simply acquainting the child with this phenomenon. Only a few words are met in beginning reading in which g is sounded as j. After stating the two rules, children may practice hearing the two sounds.

Exercise: Sounds of *G*

Teacher: "On each blank space, write *g* or *j* to show the sound that *g* represents."

_____ George	_____ goat	_____ gem	_____ game
_____ gum	_____ giant	_____ gave	_____ gentle
_____ garden	_____ general	_____ gold	_____ gun

Sounds Represented by the Letter *S*

1. The letter *s* usually represents its regular sound as heard in *said, set, sing, soap, sun.*
2. The letter *s* is sometimes sounded as *z* when it is the final sound in the word: *is, his, has, ours, please, cheese, noise.*
3. The letter *s* is sounded *sh* in *sure* and *sugar.*
4. The letter *s* is sounded *zh* in measure and treasure.

It is highly doubtful that the irregularities associated with the letter *s* have any significant impact on learning to read.

Consonants Not Sounded

A large number of English words contain one or more letters that are not sounded. In some instances, particularly when the initial letter is not sounded, it pays to learn the words as sight words. Instant word recognition and independent reading are enhanced by deliberately calling to the child's attention the more frequently occurring instances of consonants that are not sounded. We can make these generalizations:

1. In words containing double consonants, the first is sounded, the second is not.
2. In words beginning with *kn,* the *k* is usually not sounded.
3. The combination *gh* is usually not sounded when preceded by the vowel *i.*
4. In words beginning with *wr,* the *w* is usually not sounded.
5. In words ending with the syllable *ten,* the *t* is often not sounded.
6. The digraph *ck* is pronounced as *k.*
7. In words ending with *mb,* the *b* is usually not sounded.

It is doubtful that learning these rules in isolation or as a *series* of generalizations has virtue. Working with a series of stimulus words that follow one or more of the rules will help the child gain insight into the pronunciation of words. The words in Table 5–4 follow one of the generalizations.

While a given generalization may be introduced in a particular grade, it will probably have to be reviewed in subsequent grades. For some children, simple review will not be adequate, and the generalization and applications will have to be re-taught. By means of close observation or diagnosis, the teacher—at any grade level—discovers which children need help on a particular skill. She can work individually with these children or devise seatwork exercises that provide practice in the areas in which deficiencies are noted. Words of appropriate difficulty can be selected for use in various types of teaching exercises. The difficulty level of the exercises can be further controlled by the task or tasks the child is called upon to perform.

TABLE 5–4 Consonants not sounded

double consonants	kn words	gh words	wr words	-ten ending	-ck ending	-mb ending
ladder	know	sigh	write	often	sack	comb
collect	knee	light	wring	soften	neck	thumb
fellow	knight	sight	wrote	listen	block	climb
message	knew	bright	wrap	hasten	kick	bomb
roller	knit	flight	wrath	fasten	duck	lamb
summer	knife	night	wrist	glisten	clock	plumb
dinner	knock	might	wrong	moisten	black	limb
yellow	kneel	slight	wren	brighten	trick	numb
happen	knob	blight	wreck	tighten	back	crumb
kitten	known	right	wreath	frighten	pick	dumb

The purpose of the following exercises is to explain the concept that some letters in words may not represent a sound. (At this level, one need not explain in the language of linguistic science. The term *silent letters* is inaccurate, since no letters make sounds; however, to use this term with six-year-olds is not poor pedagogy.)

Exercises: Consonants Not Sounded

1. Directions: Place material on the chalkboard similar to the examples in the box. Pronounce each word. Call attention to the pair of like consonants and the fact that they represent one sound. Draw a slash through the second consonant in each pair to indicate that it is not sounded.

> su*mm*er dre*ss* le*tt*er
> Two like consonants stand for one sound.
> let/er summ/er dress/ bel/

Put words on the chalkboard that illustrate this concept (or duplicate material for seatwork). Have children cross out the letter that is not sounded.

dinner	kitten	tall
glass	cuff	barrel
ball	ladder	yellow
hidden	doll	fuzz
cross	grass	sudden
rabbit	happen	class

2. Purpose: To provide practice in sight recognition of words that contain one or more of the irregular spellings—*kn; wr; igh; mb; ph = f; gh = f.*
   Directions: Explain the irregularities of the letter combinations repeated.

Have the children note that the words in each line contain the letter pattern shown on the left. Have them practice pronouncing each word and learn these words as sight words.

kn: knew known knee knight knit knock know
(the *k* is not sounded)

wr: write wrong wreck wrote wring wrap wrist
(the *w* is not sounded)

igh: light night sight bright right fight might
(i = ī, *gh* not sounded)

mb: comb lamb thumb climb crumb bomb
(the final letter *b* is not sounded)

ph: phone photo nephew phonics autograph phrase
(*ph* represents the sound of *f*)

gh: laugh cough rough enough tough laughter
(final letters represent sound of *f*)

3. Directions: Read the following sentences. Then underline the letters *kn, wr, ph, gh, mb* each time they appear in a word.

   1. The knight knew how to write so he wrote a pamphlet.
   2. He took a right turn on the wrong light and had a wreck.
   3. The wreck was quite a sight in the bright moonlight.
   4. Phil hurt his knee and thumb taking photographs that night.
   5. If you know the alphabet and phonics you can learn to read and write.

4. Directions: (a) Pronounce all the words in each A column; (b) Strike out each "silent" consonant in the words in the A columns (the first one is done for you); (c) In the space under B, write the dictionary pronunciation of each word (to be used later in conjunction with dictionary work).

A	B	A	B
sig̶h̶t	sīt	k̶nig̶h̶t	_____
hasten	_____	glisten	_____
knew	_____	comb	_____
rabbit	_____	right	_____
thick	_____	write	_____
climb	_____	black	_____
wrote	_____	funnel	_____
dollar	_____	known	_____
debt	_____	doubt	_____
knock	_____	truck	_____
soften	_____	often	_____
summer	_____	tunnel	_____
sigh	_____	thumb	_____

5. The following exercise illustrates that unsounded letters are useful in that they produce a different word that has the same pronunciation but a different meaning from the word to which the unsounded letter is added. This letter provides a visual clue to the meaning of the new word.

In Column B, add a letter that is not sounded to each word in column A in order to produce a different word.

A	B	A	B
new	_____	night	_____
hole	_____	be	_____
our	_____	cent	_____
rap	_____	not	_____
nob	_____	plum	_____
in	_____	ring	_____

Qu-Que Combinations (*kw, k*)

Qu   The letter *q* has no sound of its own and is always followed by *u*, which in this case does not function as a vowel. The combination *qu* is pronounced *kw*—as in *quick* = *kw*ik; *quack* = *kw*ak.

Other *qu* words that might be used in teaching exercises include: *queen, quart, quiet, quit, Quaker, quake, quite, quarter, quail, quarrel.*

Que   *Que* at the end of words has the sound of *k;* usually *que* is blended with the preceding syllable:

picturesque = pĭk chûr ĕsk   plaque = plăk

antique = ăn tēk   grotesque = grō tĕsk

burlesque = bûr lĕsk   clique = klēk

opaque = ō pāk   brusque = brŭsk

critique = krĭ tēk   technique = tĕk nēk

(Note that the final syllable in *que* words is accented.)

Summary

In this chapter we build on the child's previously acquired skills of auditory-visual discrimination and deal with teaching consonant letter-sound relationships. There is a good rationale for teaching consonants in initial position in words. You now have steps for teaching single letters, blends (clusters), and digraphs, and suggestions for helping children master certain consonant letter-sound irregularities.

In general, consonant letters are quite consistent in the sounds they represent. Letters that represent only one sound include *b, d, h, j, k, l, m, n, p, r, w,* and initial *y*.

Consonants that combine are:

- *Consonant blends* (clusters), in which two or more letters blend so that sound elements of each letter are heard: *bl, bl*ack; *str, str*ing; *spl, spl*ash; *gl, gl*ide.
- *Consonant digraphs,* in which two-letter combinations result in one speech sound that is not a blend of the letters involved: *shall; white; this* (voiced *th*); *think* (unvoiced *th*); *chair, chorus* (*ch* = *k*); *chef* (*ch* = *sh*).

Some consonants and consonant combinations have irregular spellings:

- Unsounded consonants in specific combinations

1. The *k* is not sounded in *kn* (knew, knee)
2. Double consonants—only one is sounded (summer)
3. When vowel *i* precedes *gh,* the latter is not sounded (light)
4. The *w* is not sounded in *wr* at the beginning of words (writing)
5. When a word ends with the syllable *ten,* the *t* is often not sounded (often, fasten)
6. The *ck* combination is pronounced *k* (sack, clock)
7. The *b* is not sounded in *mb* at the end of words (comb, lamb)

There are two sounds for consonant *c:*

1. *c* = *k* in cake, corn, curl.
2. *c* = *s* when followed by *i, e, y* (city, cent, cycle).

There are two sounds for consonant *g:*

1. Regular sound in *go, game, gum.*
2. *g* = *j* when followed by *e, i* (gem, giant).

Other irregularities are:

1. *ph* = *f* (photo = foto; graph = graf).
2. *qu* = *kw* (quack = kwack). The letter *q* has no sound of its own. In English spellings, *q* is always followed by the letter *u.*
3. The letter *s* may be sounded in a number of ways.
   a. *s* = *s* (most common) (sell, soft, said).
   b. *s* = *z* (his = hiz; runs = runz).
   c. *s* = *sh* (sugar)
   d. *s* = *zh* (treasure)

6

Teaching Vowel Letter-Sound Relationships

Teaching the vowel letter-sound relationships is undoubtedly the most difficult and confusing part of an entire phonics program. This stems from two factors:

1. The variability of the sounds that vowel letters represent
2. The tendency to overteach certain vowel letter-sound relationships, which can be confusing rather than helpful.

We have already discussed the variability of vowel letter-sounds in Chapter 1; in essence, all the rules or generalizations that have been advanced to cover vowel letter-sounds turn out to have numerous exceptions. Nevertheless, to be successful in the decoding process, children must develop insights relative to the relationship between visual letter patterns and the sounds these patterns *usually* represent. The apparent variability in spelling and sounds should point up the fact that a number of high frequency words should be learned as sight words. A list of these sight words is provided in Table 6–1 at the end of this chapter.

Phonics Instruction as Overkill

The second problem in teaching vowel letter-sound relationships stems from the fact that teachers and schools sometimes forget the limited purpose of phonics instruction in the "learning-to-read" process. The issues are: Do we teach some "phonics" that has relatively little impact on learning to read? Do we overteach some facets of letter-sound relationships that are more appropriate for producing junior linguists rather than beginning readers?

When our goal is simply teaching children to read, some minute differences in letter-sounds need not be dealt with at all. Certain other differences can be pointed out without forcing children to spend time discriminating these sounds in lists of words. What we sometimes forget is that (in dealing with native speakers of English) children can pronounce and thus differentiate between words that contain different sound values for a given vowel letter, such as *a* in *almost, loyal, path, idea, father.* Furthermore, when children are reading for meaning, the problem diminishes in importance.

Sequence in Teaching Vowel Letter-Sounds

There are certain factors relating to the sequence of teaching skills that have served as the basis for lengthy debate. Many of these may be of little importance to children learning to read; which vowel letter-sound to teach first, whether to teach short or long sounds first, or whether to teach these two sounds concomitantly are probably not crucial issues. In fact, a quite reasonable rationale could be made for opposite views pertaining to most matters of sequence.

FIGURE 6–1 The cartoonist Malcolm Hancock suggests that phonics can be overtaught as he shows an artistic disdain for vowels.

In advocating the teaching of short vowel sounds first, it can be pointed out that a majority of the words a child meets in beginning reading contain short vowel sounds. Many of these words are single-vowel-in-medial-position words. The phonic generalization for this situation (one vowel in medial position usually has its short sound) applies in a large percentage of words met in beginning reading.

Advocacy of teaching long vowel sounds first rests on the fact that the vowel name is the long sound of the vowel (*a e i o u*). It is frequently suggested that this fact makes it easy to teach the letter-sound association.

Teaching Short Vowel Sounds

The generalizations that cover short vowel sounds deal primarily with initial single vowels and single vowels in medial position in words. Both of these vowel situations can be covered by the statement, "A single vowel that does not conclude a word usually has its short sound"; for example, *am, an, and, ant, as, ask, at, act.*

The vast majority of words covered have a vowel in medial position, however, and as a result, the following generalization is used more frequently: "A single vowel in medial position usually has its short sound," as we see when we add an initial consonant to the words for the first generalization: *ham, can, hand, pant, gas, task, bat, fact.*

We will illustrate methods for teaching the short vowel sound in medial position. To avoid repetition, we will use a teaching procedure to illustrate only one vowel sound. Obviously, any approach described here can be used to teach each of the other vowel letter-sounds that fit the generalization. (You will also find brief word lists for teaching each of the vowel letter-sounds.)

For the short sound of *a* (ă), explain to children that they have learned the sounds the consonants represent in words and that they will now practice hearing one of the sounds represented by the vowel *Aa*.

Teacher: "When we say the name of the vowel letter, we hear what is called the vowel's long sound.

"Today we are going to listen carefully and learn to hear another sound for the vowel *a*—its short sound. I am going to put some words on the board. We have studied these words before. Each of the words has the letter *a* in it. Listen to the sound the *a* has in each word."

Using this approach the generalization will evolve: "One vowel in the middle of the word usually has its short sound." It is probably not essential that each child be able to recite all the generalizations in this chapter. At this point, it might be profitable to cite other familiar words that follow the generalizations under discussion, even though all the stimulus words are not yet known as sight words.

Begin by writing these words on the chalkboard: *man, had, back, ran, cap, tag.*

1. Pronounce each word, moving your hand from left to right through the word.
2. Emphasize the sound of *a* in each word, but do not distort the sound.
3. Have the children say the words in unison, asking them to listen for the sound of ă.
4. Stress that the sound heard is called the short sound of *a.* Have the children note how this sound differs from the letter name.
5. Ask pupils how many vowels they see in each word and where the vowel is located (middle of word).

6. Have children state what sound is heard when there is one vowel in the middle of a word.[1]

7. Have children state in their own words the rule that covers this vowel situation.

Using Word Families

Some teachers find that certain children can do better in fixing the short sound of a given vowel if they see and pronounce a series of words that contain larger identical units than the vowel alone: the words *big, ship, tin, hill* have an identical unit—*i*. The words *big, pig, dig, fig;* or *hill, fill, bill, pill;* or *sit, fit, bit, kit* have rhyming units composed of several letters that have precisely the same phonic value in each word. Word families can be used both for teaching common phonic elements and for rapid recognition as sight words.

To teach the phonogram *ad,* you might begin with these words: *dad, had, sad, mad, bad, lad.* Use the steps outlined above to teach this and other identical phonogram words.

1. Pronounce each word; have children pronounce the words.

2. Stress the vowel sound heard and the visual pattern "one vowel, medial position."

Sample words are listed below for vowels *e, i, o, u.* The first column under each vowel includes words with mixed initial-final consonants; the second column presents the same final phonogram (letter-pattern) in each word.

e		*i*		*o*		*u*	
red	jet	big	hit	hop	cot	bus	bug
let	pet	tin	bit	job	not	run	rug
bell	let	hill	sit	stop	hot	cup	hug
send	bet	did	pit	log	pot	jump	jug
men	met	pig	fit	box	got	cut	mug
step	set	lift	bit	rock	lot	must	tug

Exercises: Using Context

Teacher: "Read the clue. Use one of the vowel letters *a, e, o* to spell the word that fits the clue."

Example:

Clue

spider	w__b	use *e* to spell *web*
angry	m__d	use *a* to spell *mad*
horses	tr__t	use *o* to spell *trot*

---

[1]Strictly speaking, the vowel in words such as *back, bank, trap* is not in the middle of the word. Children are usually not confused by this statement, but you can modify the generalization if you wish.

	Clue			Clue	
1.	fishing	n__t	**6.**	soda	p__p
2.	chicken	h__n	**7.**	number	t__n
3.	steal	r__b	**8.**	floor	l__mp
4.	bird's	n__st	**9.**	cry	s__b
5.	paper	b__g	**10.**	lion's	d__n

Teacher: "Now use one of the vowel letters *i, u, e* to spell the word."

	Clue			Clue	
1.	chewy	g__m	**6.**	fish	sw__m
2.	color	r__d	**7.**	scissors	c__t
3.	tops	sp__n	**8.**	rings	b__ll
4.	plane	j__t	**9.**	fruit	pl__m
5.	ruler	k__ng	**10.**	large	b__g

Teacher: "Read the clue. Write the vowel that completes the word that fits the clue."

Example:
Sleep on this b__d.

Clue			Clue	
It's large	b__g		Can ring it	b__ll
Paper sack	b__g		Can throw it	b__ll
An insect	b__g		Lives on the farm	b__ll
To keep asking for	b__g		A boy's name	B__ll

Teacher: "Read the clue. Write the word that fits the clue."

Example:
The pig is in the _____. (pin, pen)

Clue			
Do you like corn on the	_____?	cab	cob
John said, "I can read the	_____."	mop	map
The cat drank milk from the	_____.	cap	cup
Cats and dogs are	_____.	pots	pets
A baby bear is a	_____.	cab	cub

Teacher: "Each sentence has two blanks. One of the words *pig* or *pen* will fit in each space. Study each sentence and write the correct words."

Example:
The (*pig*) is in the (*pen*).

1. Put the _____ in the _____.
2. Will the _____ hold the _____?
3. The _____ will hold the _____.

4. The _____ should be in the _____.
5. The _____ is for the _____.
6. Is the _____ in the _____?
7. The _____ belongs in the _____.
8. It is time to _____ up the _____.

Teacher: "Read each sentence. One of the words at the right fits in the blank space. Write the correct word in the blank space. The only difference in the words is the vowel letter."

Example:

The _____ was many years old. click
clock

1. There was a _____ on the beach. crab
crib

2. The _____ was full of coal. trick
truck

3. John was able to _____ the word. spell
spill

4. Spot is a _____ dog. smell
small

5. _____ the letter in the mail box. drop
drip

Exercises: Fun with Language

Teacher: "Fill every blank space with a vowel. The context will help you pick the right vowel."
Clue:
Suzy sings a lot.
Will she sing a song again if she has just sung that song?

1. Just ask Suzy and she will s___ng any s___ng.
2. Once she s___ng a very pretty s___ng.
3. Later, someone asked her to s___ng that s___ng again.
4. She said, "I just s___ng that s___ng."
5. I should not s___ng a s___ng that I have just s___ng.
6. Was Suzy right not to s___ng that s___ng again?
7. Would you s___ng a s___ng you had just s___ng?
8. If you have just s___ng a s___ng and you want to s___ng it again, s___ng it!

Buckets and Blank Spaces

Teacher: "Note that each underlined word has the same three letters. To complete each word you must add a vowel. Which vowel goes where? As you read the sentence the context will indicate where to add *a–e–i–u.*"

1. First, you f___ll the bucket f___ll of water.
2. Don't f___ll while carrying a bucket f___ll of water.
3. If you f___ll the bucket might not be f___ll.
4. He f___ll, then he had to f___ll the bucket again.
5. Don't f___ll if you want a f___ll bucket.

Teacher: "In each sentence below, two words need a vowel. The context will help you decide which words fit. Write the vowel letter to complete each word."

Set 1

Use only the vowels *u–i–e*

1. Is the b___g very b___g?
2. S___t the basket down and come s___t by me.
3. Don't d___g where we d___g yesterday.
4. That t___n cup cost t___n cents.
5. She asked h___m, "Can you h___m this song?"
6. You write with a p___n, not with a p___n.

Set 2

Use only the vowels *a–o–i.*

1. The c___t was asleep on the c___t.
2. "Watch out," said Joe, "the p___t is very h___t."
3. I want to s___t where we s___t yesterday.
4. Ask h___m if he wants a h___m sandwich.
5. Put the b___g dish in the paper b___g.
6. When the weather is h___t you should wear a h___t.

Minimal Contrast Vowels

Practice in associating vowel letter forms with the short sound they represent can be presented in many ways. The examples start with contrasting two vowel sounds and gradually move through all vowels in medial position.

Contrasting two vowel sounds.   As soon as two vowel sounds have been introduced, the difference between them can be stressed.

1. Write pairs of words on the chalkboard:

bat–bet	mat–met	pat–pet	sat–set
man–men	tan–ten	bad–bed	lad–led

2. Pronounce these words, inviting children to "listen to the difference in the vowel sounds heard in the middle of the words."
3. Have children pronounce the pairs of words, noting the vowel letter form and the sound it represents.

   The short sounds of *e* and *i* often pose special difficulty because of either poor auditory discrimination or dialectical differences in pronunciation. The following pairs of words, identical except for the vowel *i–e*, can be used in both auditory and visual drill:

led-lid	big-beg	pig-peg	wit-wet
pin-pen	tin-ten	din-den	met-mitt
bed-bid	pep-pip	bet-bit	rid-red
lit-let	pit-pet	sit-set	hem-him

Various exercises using different modes of presentation can be built from pairs of words such as these:

u–i	*u–e*	*a–u*	*o–u*
bug — big	bug — beg	bag — bug	cot — cut
but — bit	but — bet	bat — but	hot — hut
hut — hit	nut — net	cat — cut	not — nut
dug — dig	hum — hem	cap — cup	hog — hug

e–o	*a–o*	*a–i*	*i–o*
get — got	cat — cot	lap — lip	hip — hop
let — lot	hat — hot	nap — nip	tip — top
net — not	pat — pot	rap — rip	Tim — Tom
pet — pot	rat — rot	tap — tip	hit — hot

Seeing and sounding drill.   After all short vowel letter-sounds have been introduced, exercise material can help children fix the visual-auditory relationship involved in the single vowel in medial position generalization. To use the following material, children should be told that the words in each line are exactly the same except for the vowel letter-sound:

1. "Listen for the difference (vowel sound) in each word."
2. "If the word is underlined, it is a nonsense word you haven't met—but you *can* pronounce it."
3. "Read across each line of words."

a	*e*	*i*	*o*	*u*
bag	beg	big	bog	bug
→	→			
lad	led	lid	lod	lud
pat	pet	pit	pot	pud
dask	desk	disk	dosk	dusk
jag	jeg	jig	jog	jug
ham	hem	him	hom	hum
fan	fen	fin	fon	fun
Nat	net	nit	not	nut
lack	leck	lick	lock	luck
sap	sep	sip	sop	sup

Exercise: Blend and Say

Teacher: "Each word has a blank space. A vowel letter is shown above each blank space. Think of the sound of the vowel letter and say each word."

a	e	i	o	u
b__t	b__d	h__t	h__p	f__n
a	e	i	o	u
c__n	j__t	p__g	l__g	b__s
e	u	o	i	a
m__n	g__m	c__t	s__x	f__t
i	o	a	u	e
d__g	m__p	r__t	f__n	l__g

Exercise: Change the Vowel

Teacher: "Change the vowel and make a naming word for 'something living' using the vowels (a–e–i–o–u)."

Example:
cot – cat; pep – pup.

dig	d__g	big	b__g
dock	d__ck	limb	l__mb
pit	p__t	crib	cr__b
cot	c__t	bell	b__ll
fix	f__x	peg	p__g

Exercises: Write and Say

These exercises can be presented in many different ways, including the chalkboard and duplicated exercises.
Teacher: "Put the vowel *a* in each blank space below. Then pronounce the word."

t__p	b__d
n__p	d__d
l__p	h__d
m__p	m__d
c__p	s__d

Teacher: "Put the vowel *e* in each blank space below. Then pronounce the word."

m__n	l__t
p__n	n__t

```
        d__n      p__t
        h__n      j__t
        t__n      b__t
```

Teacher: "Put the vowel *i* in each blank space below. Pronounce the word."

```
        p__n      h__t
        t__n      b__t
        b__n      s__t
        f__n      f__t
        s__n      p__t
```

Teacher: "Put the vowel *u* in each blank space below. Pronounce the word."

```
        r__g      r__n
        j__g      s__n
        h__g      f__n
        t__g      g__n
        d__g      b__n
```

Teacher: "Add a vowel to make a word. Only *one* vowel fits in each word."

Examples:

```
        w__b      a–e–i–o–u      (e)
        f__sh     a–e–i–o–u      (i)
```

1. y__s	7. gl__d	13. k__ss
2. v__m	8. r__ch	14. pl__n
3. sk__m	9. y__t	15. b__s
4. cl__b	10. s__ch	16. m__lk
5. p__nd	11. d__st	17. s__nt
6. k__g	12. d__t	18. n__st

Combining Teaching of Initial-Medial Vowel Sounds

Some teachers prefer to teach the short sound of initial and medial vowels simultaneously. The procedure can be much the same as for the medial-vowel situation; however, the generalization that emerges will be stated differently. To illustrate this concept, place a number of stimulus words on the board.

```
        a          a
        am         ham
        ask        task
        at         bat
```

and	sand
as	gas
act	fact
an	pan

Words in the first column contain one vowel (initial), and the short sound is heard. Words in the second column contain one vowel (medial), and the short sound is heard. As children see and hear the letter-sound relationship, the generalization will emerge: "One vowel that does not come at the end of a word usually has its short sound."

The Long Vowel (Glided) Letter-Sounds

In teaching the long vowel letter-sounds, keep in mind that children differentiate these sounds when they process *or* use oral language. In the reading process, teaching the long vowel letter-sounds focuses primarily on having the child recognize several visual patterns and associate these with the sound they characteristically represent.

Using Visual Patterns as Cues to Sounding

Despite the large number of exceptions to any generalizations advanced to cover vowel letter-sounds, certain visual cues must be heeded. We will look at these major patterns:

Two adjacent vowels: particularly m*ee*t s*ea*t c*oa*t s*ai*l

Medial vowel and final *e*: r*o*p*e* c*a*p*e* c*u*t*e* t*i*r*e*

Single vowel that concludes a word: g*o* m*e*

How *y* functions at end of words: m*y* ma*y*

Two adjacent vowels are covered by the generalization: "When two vowels come together, the first one usually has its long sound and the second is not sounded."

Data from studies of a large sample of words met in elementary reading materials indicate that this generalization actually applies to less than half the words that meet the two-vowel criteria; however, the generalization held fairly consistently for the *ee*, *oa*, *ai*, and *ea* patterns. Studies revealed the percentage of instances in which the two-vowel rule applies: *ee*, 98%; *oa*, 97%; *ai*, 64%; *ea*, 66%; all two-vowel situations combined, 48% (Oaks, 1952; Clymer, 1963).

In the following examples, teaching does not start with a statement of generalizations but with material that emphasizes the visual patterns (*oa–ee–ai–ea*). The patterns are linked to the sound heard in words and permit the children to discover the relationship and arrive at the generalization.

1. Place a column of *oa* words on the board: *boat, coat, load, road, soak.*
2. Pronounce each word, emphasizing the long ō sound.
3. Have children note the visual pattern of the two vowels.

4. Point out that in each word, "you hear the long sound of the first vowel and the second vowel is not sounded" (this may be illustrated as in the right-hand column).

boat	bōa̸t
coat	cōa̸t
load	lōa̸d
road	rōa̸d
soak	sōa̸k

A similar procedure can be followed to introduce the patterns *ai, ea,* and *ee:*

ai		*ea*		*ee*	
chain	chāi̸n	beat	bēa̸t	feed	fēe̸d
mail	māi̸l	dream	drēa̸m	seed	sēe̸d
wait	wāi̸t	leaf	lēa̸f	keep	kēe̸p
rain	rāi̸n	teach	tēa̸ch	queen	quēe̸n
paid	pāi̸d	seat	sēa̸t	steel	stēe̸l

Teaching Short and Long Sounds Together

Some teachers prefer to present short and long sounds simultaneously. This procedure permits the child to see both patterns (single and double vowel letters) and to contrast the sounds in familiar words. Material can be presented in two- or three-step fashion.

Teacher: "Today we want to practice hearing the difference between two sounds of the vowel letter *a.* In the first column, all words have one vowel letter. In the second column each word has two vowels together."

ran	rain
pad	paid
bat	bait
lad	laid
pal	pail
mad	maid
pan	pain

1. Pronounce the words in the first column; then have children read these words.
2. Have pupils note:
   a. Each word has one vowel.
   b. The vowel is in the middle of the word.
   c. The short sound (ă) of the vowel is heard.
3. Repeat the procedure for the words in the second column, having the children note:
   a. Each word contains the vowel pattern *ai.*
   b. They say and hear the letter *a* (ā).
   c. They do not sound or hear the second vowel letter.

The three-step approach permits the child to see the process of adding a second vowel. This produces a new word containing two vowels that represent the long vowel sound heard.

One vowel	Add *i*	New word	
ă	↓	long ā	
ran	ra*i*n	rā*i*n	(second vowel
pad	pa d	pāid	not sounded)
bat	ba t	bāit	
lad	la d	lāid	
pal	pa l	pāil	
mad	ma d	māid	
pan	pa n	pāin	

These words can be used to teach the other two-vowel patterns (*ee, ea, oa*):

ă	ēē	ĕ	ēā	ŏ	ōā
bet	beet	set	seat	cot	coat
met	meet	men	mean	got	goat
fed	feed	bet	beat	rod	road
step	steep	bed	bead	Tod	toad
pep	peep	met	meat	cost	coast

Exercises: Using Context

Teacher: "Read the clue. Complete the word that fits the clue. Use one of the vowel patterns *a–e, i–e, o–e* to spell the word."

Example:

	Clue		
	Opening in fence:	g__t__	(*a–e* for *gate*)
	A pretty flower:	r__s__	(*o–e* for *rose*)

Clue		*Clue*	
ten cents:	d__m__	sticky stuff:	p__st__
a brief letter:	n__t__	a two-wheeler:	b__k__
a number:	n__n__	a body of water:	l__k__
glass in window:	p__n__	a funny story:	j__k__
where there's fire:	sm__k__	go fly a:	k__t__

Teacher: "Now use one of the vowel patterns *ai, ee, ea* to spell the word."

Clue:		*Clue*	
used for thinking:	br_____n	a lady ruler:	qu_____n
falls from clouds:	r_____n	when it hurts:	p_____n
a vegetable:	b_____t	path in woods:	tr_____l
to cure the sick:	h_____l	along the ocean:	b_____ch
not very strong:	w_____k	back of foot:	h_____l

Teacher: "The two words *not* and *note* fit in the two blanks in each sentence. Study each sentence and fill in the blanks."

1. He did _____ see the _____.
2. The _____ was _____ seen.
3. Why did he _____ see the _____?
4. Was the _____ seen or _____?
5. No, the _____ was _____ seen.

Teacher: "One of the words *met* or *meet* will fit in each blank space. Complete each sentence."

Examples:
Did you _____meet_____ the new teacher?
Yes, we _____met_____ yesterday.

1. _____ me at the ball game.
2. They _____ last year at camp.
3. The boys _____ at the track _____.
4. She will _____ us at four o'clock.
5. He said, " _____ me where we _____ last time."

Teacher: "All these sentences contain two blank spaces. Each word following a sentence will fit in one blank space. You decide which one."

Example:

When the _____rain_____ started, he _____ran_____ home.

ran
rain

1. They _____ at the _____ market.

met
meat

2. Some of the _____ were _____.

mean
men

3. Do not _____ it where you _____ it before.

hid
hide

4. The doctor said, "You _____ walk with a _____."

cane
can

5. She _____ some of the people _____.

mad
made

Exercises: Fun with Language

Teacher: "In each sentence, three words need a pair of vowels. Write *ee, ea,* or *oa* in each blank space."

1. T_____ch children to k_____p off the r_____d.
2. You don't f_____d m_____t to a g_____t.
3. We n_____d a r_____l good rain to s_____k the ground.
4. It's hard to k_____p a c_____l mine cl_____n.
5. We n_____d some m_____t and a l_____f of bread.
6. I f_____l like eating v_____l r_____st and pie.
7. It was m_____n to k_____p the g_____t tied up.

Teacher: "Each sentence below contains two words with missing vowels. The *clue* tells you which vowel patterns will fit. Read the sentence to learn *where* they fit."

Set 1

Clues to use: *ee, oa, ea*

1. M_____t me at the m_____t market.
2. He sat near the r_____d to r_____d his book.
3. The doctor said, "This will h_____l your injured h_____l."
4. She took a last p_____k at the high mountain p_____k.

Set 2

Clues to use: *ea, ai, oa*

5. If we s_____l to the island we may see the s_____l.
6. The guide said, "Put the b_____t in the b_____t."
7. The g_____t walked with a funny g_____t.
8. Is the r_____l made of r_____l walnut wood?

Two Vowels One of Which Is Final e

The generalization for this CVCV pattern is: "In two-vowel words ending with *e,* the final *e* is not sounded and the first vowel *usually* represents its long sound." Clymer (1963) found that the pronunciation of 60 percent of the "final e words" in his sample were governed by this generalization. Again, material can be presented so that children see the pattern, hear the long vowel sound, and arrive at the generalization.

1. Write on the board words that have a single vowel in medial position. (Choose words to which a final *e* may be added to form a new word.)
2. In an adjacent column, print these "final *e*" words.
3. Have children pronounce these pairs of words, listening to the difference in the vowel sounds.

Stress the visual pattern (vowel + *e*), and guide children in verbalizing the generalization—the final *e* is not sounded and the first vowel usually has its long sound. (You can use diacritical marks as shown in Column C.)

A	B	C
hat	hate	hāte̸
hid	hide	hīde̸
past	paste	pāste̸
pal	pale	pāle̸
cut	cute	cūte̸
plan	plane	plāne̸
rat	rate	rāte̸
pin	pine	pīne̸
strip	stripe	strīpe̸
rid	ride	rīde̸

The final e rule: When a word has two vowels and ends with e, the first vowel *usually* has its long sound.

Exercises: Vowel Sounds

Teacher: "The sentences below have two underlined words ending with e. Circle any underlined word that has a long vowel sound."

1. When will the boys come home?
2. Does bone rhyme with none?
3. Have you ever seen the cave?
4. "Please give me five dozen," he said.
5. The dog is done with the bone.
6. I love to cook on the new stove.
7. Does the word some rhyme with home?
8. Later the pretty stone was gone.

Teacher: "Write down all of the underlined words which do not have a long vowel sound. These are exceptions to the final e rule."

_____ _____ _____ _____

_____ _____ _____ _____

Teacher: "In each sentence, two words need a vowel. The same vowel letter fits in each blank. One word will have its short sound; the other will have the long sound. Write in the vowel that makes sense."

1. John said, "I would h___te to lose my new h___t."
2. Do n___t forget to leave a n___te.
3. I h___pe the rabbit will not h___p on the flowers.
4. His friend P___te has a p___t turtle.

5. A r__t can run at a very fast r__te.
6. Their job was to c__t out some c__te cartoons.
7. Under the p__ne tree, he found a pretty p__n.
8. If you h__d there once, don't h__de there again.

Exercise: Fun with Language

Teacher: "Every word with a blank space ends with *e*. Each blank space needs a vowel. This vowel will have its long vowel sound. Complete all of the words so that the sentence makes sense."

1. D__ve, M__ke, and K__te m__de plans for a picnic.
2. M__ke will b__ke a c__ke.
3. K__te will t__ke a l__me and lemon drink.
4. D__ve will t__ke a pl__te of r__pe fruit.
5. Later, D__ve and M__ke met K__te at the l__ke.
6. She r__de her b__ke; she l__kes to r__de it.
7. They will w__de in the l__ke, then t__ke a h__ke.

Single Final Vowels

When the only vowel in a word comes at the end of the word, it usually has its long sound. There probably are enough high frequency words covered by this generalization to justify calling it to children's attention.

1. Place on the board words that contain one vowel in final position.
2. Have pupils pronounce each word, noting the vowel at end of word and sound it represents.
3. Invite children to supply a rule covering these words (one final vowel has long sound).

In words that end with *y* and which contain no other vowel, the *y* functions as a vowel. In these words the *y* is sounded as long ī (e.g., *my, by, try, fly, cry, dry, sky, shy*).

AY at the end of words has the sound of long ā.   Children have learned that *y* functions as a vowel when it ends a word that has no other vowel letter. Here they learn that *y* following the vowel *a* fits a generalization learned previously: "When two vowels come together, the first usually has its long sound."

1. Place a few stimulus words on the board.
2. Lead the children in pronouncing these words.

3. Focus attention on the visual pattern *ay* and on the resulting sound of long *ā*.
4. Other words that fit this pattern: *play, hay, ray, pray, sway, jay, stray, gray, away, tray.*

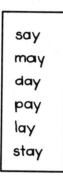

Sound of y at end of longer words. When *y* concludes a word of two or more syllables, it has the long sound of *e* heard in: hob *by*, win *dy*, fog *gy*, luc *ky*, jol *ly*, fun *ny*, hap *py*, mer *ry*, noi *sy*, rus *ty*. Other words to use in teaching exercises are *badly, angry, plenty, honestly, closely, beauty, mainly, guilty, history, lively, nasty, January, partly, ready, seventy, rocky, penny, muddy, simply, sorry, jelly, nearly, costly, sleepy.*

Exceptions to Vowel Rules Previously Taught

There is no vowel rule or generalization that will apply in all situations. When exceptions to a given rule occur, they may be taught as sight words or a new rule can be devised to cover the exception. It has been suggested that children not be burdened with rules that have limited applications. Different teachers will, of course, arrive at different conclusions as to which generalizations should be included in phonics instruction. Some exceptions to a given rule occur with such frequency as to merit calling the child's attention to the exceptions.

For instance, one of the most useful phonic generalizations we have discussed states: "One vowel in medial position usually has its short sound." There are several series of words that meet the criterion of one vowel in medial position but in which the vowel has its long sound. For example, the vowel *o* followed by *ld* or *lt* usually has the long sound: *bold, mold, gold, sold, hold, told, fold, cold, colt, bolt, volt, jolt.* Also, the vowel *i* followed by *nd, gh,* or *ld* frequently has the long sound: *find, blind, behind, mind, kind, light, fight, sight, right, wild, mild, child.*

Two Adjacent Vowels

The generalization covering two adjacent vowels ("first is usually long, second not sounded") has some exceptions in the patterns *oa, ai, ee, ea.* While children are learning the words that follow the rule, they should also understand that exceptions will occur, such as *been, again, against, aisle, said, bread, break, head, dead, heart, steak, broad.* There are many more exceptions found among other two-vowel patterns, including these:

ei	ou	ie	au	ui–ue–ua
their	could	chief	caught	build
weigh	enough	field	laugh	guide
eight	rough	friend	fault	quiet
neighbor	should	piece	haunt	guess
vein	would	quiet	taught	guest
freight	touch	view	daughter	guard
rein	double	believe	haul	usual

Medial Vowel Plus Final *e*

Since a number of frequently met words, particularly *o* + *e* words, do not follow the rule, some teachers prefer to deal with this fact rather than ignore it. Teachers might point out several exceptions, noting that applying the above rule will not help in solving the words: *come, done, none, move, have, were, there, one, some, gone, love, glove, give, sense, where, lose.*

Vowel Sounds Affected by *R*

A vowel (or vowels) followed by the letter *r* results in a blended sound which is neither the short nor the long sound of the vowel. This phonic fact—as it relates to learning to read—is probably not extremely important, however, calling the child's attention to this role of the letter *r* is a justifiable procedure. Since the child uses and understands hundreds of words that include a vowel followed by *r*, this is not a particularly difficult fact to teach. More important, the child will have mastered several such words as sight words, and these can serve as examples when the generalization is introduced. These are some of the more common vowel *-r* words for use in board work or seatwork exercises:

-ar		-er	-or
car	yard	her	for
farm	park	person	corn
march	card	term	storm
part	far	serve	horn
star	smart	ever	short
dark	arm	certain	north
hard	bark	berth	horse
barn	tar	herd	corner
start	spark	under	form

The spelling *ir* is usually pronounced *ûr* (bird = bûrd), except when followed by a final *e* (fire): *bird, dirt, firm, third, fir, thirst, girl, first, sir, shirt, birth, stir.*

A Followed by L, LL, W, and *U*

The letter *a* has the sound *ô* (*aw*) when it is followed by *l, ll, w, u;* for example:

talk	all	wall	saw	claw	haul
walk	tall	fall	draw	straw	because
salt	small	call	lawn	drawn	fault
halt	hall	ball	drawn	jaw	Paul

The *oo* Sounds

Explaining the sounds of *oo* is much more complicated than actually learning to arrive at the correct pronunciation of the frequently used words that contain this letter combination. Most words containing *oo* are pronounced in one of two ways:

The sound heard in b$\overline{oo}$ and b$\overline{oo}$t

The sound heard in b$\breve{oo}$k and f$\breve{oo}$t

Native speakers of English do not confuse these sounds while speaking or listening. When reading for meaning, the child will not confuse the medial sounds heard in the two words used in each of these sentences:

The boot is larger than the foot.

The food is very good.

The beginning reader may not consciously note that the sounds are different because he never substitutes one for the other. Practice in hearing differences can be provided by having the child tell which of the following pairs of words rhyme:

cool-pool	food-good	soon-moon
boot-foot	book-look	look-hook
hoot-foot	wood-good	boot-hoot

The markings $\overline{oo}$ and $\breve{oo}$ may help children note the differences between these sounds, as in these sentences:

The b$\overline{oo}$t is larger than the f$\breve{oo}$t.

The m$\overline{oo}$se drank from the c$\overline{oo}$l p$\overline{oo}$l.

He t$\breve{oo}$k a l$\breve{oo}$k at the br$\breve{oo}$k.

In the final analysis, it is the context that helps the child arrive at the correct pronunciation. For convenience in creating board or seatwork exercises, here are some $\overline{oo}$ and $\breve{oo}$ words:

		$\overline{oo}$		$\breve{oo}$	
b$\overline{oo}$	s$\overline{oo}$n	m$\overline{oo}$n	b$\overline{oo}$st	b$\breve{oo}$k	f$\breve{oo}$t
c$\overline{oo}$l	t$\overline{oo}$l	br$\overline{oo}$m	l$\overline{oo}$p	g$\breve{oo}$d	t$\breve{oo}$k

fōod	bōot	pōol	hōot	stŏod	lŏok
rōom	bōon	lōose	mōose	shŏok	crŏok
tōoth	zōo	rōot	prōof	wŏod	hŏok

A few *oo* words are neither *ōo* or *ŏo*, such as *blood* (blŭd), *door* (dōr), *flood* (flŭd), and *floor* (flōr). These should be taught as sight words.

Diphthongs

Diphthongs are two adjacent vowels, each of which contributes to the sound heard. The diphthongs discussed here are *ou, ow, oi, oy.* In pronouncing diphthongs, the two vowel sounds are blended, as in h*ou*se, *ow*l, *oi*l, b*oy.*

1. The diphthongs *oi* and *oy* have the same sound (b*oy* = b*oi*; b*oil* = b*oi*l).
2. The diphthongs *ou* and *ow* have the same sound (pl*ow* = pl*ou*; n*ow* = n*ou*).
3. The above vowel combinations are diphthongs only when pronounced as in h*ou*se, *ow*l, *oi*l, b*oy.*

Teaching Diphthong Sounds

1. Place several words on the board that illustrate the diphthong sound *oy* (column A).
2. In column B, change the spelling to *oi,* and in column C, add a final consonant to form a known word.

A		B		C
boy	→	*boi*	→	boil
toy	→	*toi*	→	toil
joy	→	*joi*	→	join
coy	→	*coi*	→	coin

3. Pronounce the words across each line, emphasizing that the *oy–oi* spellings represent the same sounds.
4. Point out that each vowel letter contributes to the sound heard.
5. Have children note that these vowel patterns do not follow the "two-vowel rule," that is, the first vowel long, the second not sounded.

   Teaching that the diphthong sounds *ou* and *ow* represent the same sound may be done as follows:

1. Have children pronounce these pairs of words, noting that *ou* and *ow* represent the same sound.

*ow*l	f*ou*l
cr*ow*d	cl*ou*d
f*ow*l	gr*ou*nd

2. Place other *ou–ow* stimulus words on the board. In pronouncing the words in columns A and B, help children note the vowel letters represent the same sound.

```
    A              B
   how            out
   howl           foul
   town           found
   drown          ground
   round          clown
   sound          crown
```

Here is a list of diphthong words to use in board or seatwork drill:

cow	owl	mouse	mouth	boil	boy
how	gown	sound	proud	coin	toy
brown	howl	loud	shout	toil	oyster
tower	brow	couch	found	joint	joy
crown	town	south	count	soil	Troy
powder	fowl	ground	bound	moist	employ

Teaching *ow* as Long Sound of *o*

In a number of English words, the *ow* combination has the sound of long ō. You can use these steps to teach the sound.

1. The letter combination *ow* has two sounds: the diphthong sound heard in "plow" and the ō heard in "snow."

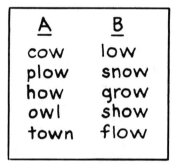

```
  A       B
 cow     low
 plow    snow
 how     grow
 owl     show
 town    flow
```

2. Pronounce the words in column A, with pupils listening to the sound of *ow*.
3. Pronounce pairs of words (*cow, low*) with pupils listening to contrasting sounds.
4. Have pupils pronounce the words.
5. Point out that as words are read in context, the proper sound becomes obvious since the children know these words.

Homonyms

Homonyms are words that have the same pronunciation but different spellings and meanings. These words involve both structural and phonic analysis skills. Some homonyms follow one of the generalizations we have already introduced; many do not. For example, the rule "two vowels together—the first is long, and the second is not sounded" applies to both words in the following pairs: *meet, meat; see, sea; week, weak.*

Sometimes the rule applies to one word in a pair, and the final -e rule applies to the other word: *road, rode; sail, sale; pain, pane.*

Some pairs involve unsounded consonants: *rap, wrap; new, knew; our, hour.*

Other examples of phonic irregularities are *wait, weight; wood, would; ate, eight; piece, peace.* The following exercises may be used or adapted to help children recognize homonyms that have irregular spellings.

Exercises: Working with Homonyms

1. Directions: Explain the concept of homonyms (words pronounced the same but having different spellings and meanings). Have children pronounce the pairs of words at the left and answer the questions by writing *yes* or *no.*

	Same Spelling?	*Same Sound?*
there—their	_____	_____
ate—eight	_____	_____
two—to	_____	_____
would—wood	_____	_____
one—won	_____	_____
I--eye	_____	_____
some—sum	_____	_____
by—buy	_____	_____
our—hour	_____	_____
do—due	_____	_____

2. Matching Homonyms
   Directions: Draw a line from the word in Column A to the word in Column B that is pronounced the same.

A	B	A	B
won	no	knot	sun
know	our	blue	pare
so	eight	made	not
pole	some	son	I
hour	one	eye	sea
ate	sew	pear	maid
sum	poll	see	blew

3. Match and Write Homonyms
Directions: Explain that each word in the box is pronounced like one of the words below the box. Children are to write the correct word on the blank space.

				Clue Box			
eight	one	weigh	sew	some	would	wait	hole

so	_____	ate	_____
won	_____	sum	_____
way	_____	wood	_____
whole	_____	weight	_____

These are some common homonyms to use in board or seatwork exercises:

beat — beet	maid — made	pair — pare
know — no	I — eye	mail — male
hear — here	hair — hare	steel — steal
there — their	by — buy	waist — waste
sun — son	fair — fare	one — won
whole — hole	dear — deer	some — sum
oh — owe	not — knot	tail — tale

Using Context

Teacher: "Two words follow each clue. These are homonyms — words pronounced the same but spelled differently. Read the clue and write the correct word in the blank space."

Example:

big price cut	_____	sail	<u>sale</u>

	Clue			
1.	the ears do it:	_____	here	hear
2.	part of a window:	_____	pain	pane
3.	seven days in a:	_____	week	weak
4.	the eyes do it:	_____	sea	see
5.	an odd-shaped fruit:	_____	pair	pear
6.	fuel for a fireplace:	_____	wood	would
7.	a vegetable:	_____	beat	beet

    8. top of a mountain: _____   peek   peak

    9. back part of the foot: _____   heal   heel

   10. cars move on it: _____   rode   road

Teacher: "One of the words *weak* or *week* will fit in each blank space. Study each sentence and fill in the blanks."

Example:
There are seven days in a _____. (week)
He felt very _____ after the fever. (weak)

1. John was sick last _____.

2. He feels _____ this _____.

3. John has felt _____ since last _____.

4. Next _____ , John will not be _____.

5. How did John feel last _____?

Teacher: "Each sentence below has an <u>underlined</u> word and a blank space _____ . In the blank space, write a homonym for the underlined word."

Examples:
We can be at <u>our</u> house in an _____. (hour)
Who <u>knew</u> about the _____ plans? (new)

1. The team <u>won</u> only _____ game.

2. <u>Eight</u> of the boys _____ all of the chicken.

3. _____ house is over <u>there</u>.

4. <u>Would</u> you please bring in some _____.

5. You can _____ the ocean if you come over <u>here</u>.

Teacher: "Each of these sentences has two missing words. The words *our* and *hour* will fit in each sentence. Where does each word fit?"

Example:
There was a one _____ meeting at _____ house.
Using the context of the sentence you would write:
There was a one *hour* meeting at *our* house.

1. _____ game will start in one _____.

2. In about an _____ _____ game will start.

3. Will it take an _____ to play _____ game?

4. We can play _____ game in less than an _____.

Teacher: "The words *mail* and *male* are homonyms. Homonyms are words that are pronounced the _____, but have different _____. Each of these sentences has two missing words. The words *mail* and *male* will fit in each sentence. Where does each word fit?"

Example:
A _____ or a female may bring the _____.
Note that the context helps you get it right.
A *male* or a female may bring the *mail.*

1. When a _____ delivers the _____ he is called a mailman.

2. A _____ delivering the _____ is not a "maleman."

3. _____ can be delivered by a _____ or a female.

4. Who is the _____ delivering the _____ today?

5. That _____ delivering the _____ is Charlie.

The Schwa Sound

In a large number of words of more than one syllable, there is a diminished stress on one of the syllables. The sound of the vowel in these unstressed syllables undergoes a slight change, referred to as a *softening* of the vowel sound. This softened vowel sound is called the *schwa* sound, and it is represented by the symbol ə.

All of the vowels are represented by the schwa sound, as illustrated by each of the italicized vowels in these words:

bedl*a*m	=	bed'ləm
beat*e*n	=	bē'tən
beaut*i*ful	=	bū'tə fəl
beck*o*n	=	bek'ən

In other words, if vowels were interchanged in unstressed syllables, the spellings would change but the sound heard would remain the same for the different vowels. For instance, read both of these sentences without stressing the second syllable in any word:

A. "Button, button, who has the button?"
B. "Buttun, buttan, who has the butten?"

If, in reading sentence B, you give each second syllable the same stress as it was given in the word directly above it, the sounds remain constant. Thus, teaching the schwa sound in the initial stages of reading would have little impact on one's ability to sound out words. Once the child begins to use a dictionary that utilizes the schwa symbol, ə, however, these points should be explained.

Sight-Word List

Table 6–1 is a list of words, most of which are met in primary reading, that illustrates irregular spellings. From the standpoint of spoken language, all words are phonetic; however, the spellings of these words (visual patterns) are such that the more common phonic generalizations learned in beginning reading will not apply.

TABLE 6–1: Sight-word list (Words with irregular spellings—confusion between letters seen and sounds heard)

above	could	ghost	love	quiet	together
across	couple	give			ton
again	cousin	gives	machine	ranger	tongue
against	cruel	gloves	many	ready	too
aisle	curve	gone	measure	really	touch
already		great	might	right	two
another	dead	guard	mild	rough	
answer	deaf	guess	million		use
anxious	debt	guest	mind	said	usual
any	desire	guide	minute	says	
	do		mischief	school	vein
bear	does	have	mother	science	very
beautiful	done	head	move	scissors	view
beauty	don't	heart	Mr.	sew	
because	double	heaven	Mrs.	shoe	was
been	doubt	heavy		should	wash
behind	dove	here	neighbor	sign	weather
believe	dozen	high	neither	snow	weight
bind			night	soften	were
both	early	idea	none	soldier	what
bough	earn	Indian		some	where
bread	eight	instead	ocean	someone	who
break	enough	isle	of	something	whom
bright	eye		office	sometime	whose
brought	eyes	key	often	son	wild
build		kind	oh	soul	wind
built	father	knee	once	special	wolf
bury	fence	knew	one	spread	woman
busy	field	knife	onion	square	women
buy	fight	know	only	steak	won
	find		other	straight	would
calf	folks	language	ought	sure	wrong
captain	four	laugh		sword	
caught	freight	laughed	patient		you
chief	friend	leather	piece	their	young
child	front	library	pretty	there	your
clothes		light	pull	they	
colt	garage	lion	purpose	though	
coming	get	live	push	thought	
cough	getting	lived	put	to	

Summary

There is considerable variability in the sound of vowels and vowel combinations in English. This increases the difficulty of teaching or learning vowel sounds. The sequence in which vowel sounds are taught—that is, whether to teach long or short sounds first or which vowels to teach first—is probably not a significant issue. The teaching procedures in this chapter are meant to be illustrative rather than prescriptive.

Some generalizations covering vowel situations include these:

- A single vowel in medial position in a word or syllable usually has its short sound (*man, bed, fit*).

Exceptions:

The vowel *o* followed by *ld* or *lt* usually has its long sound: *sōld, cōld, bōlt.*

The vowel *i* followed by *nd, gh, ld* often has its long sound: *fīnd, līght, chīld.*

The vowel *a = aw* when it is followed by *l, ll, w, u: walk, fall, draw, because.*

A vowel followed by the letter *r* results in a blended sound which is neither the short nor long sound of the vowel: *car, her, for.*

The spelling *ir* is usually pronounced *ur (bird = burd),* except when followed by a final *e (fire).*

(These exceptions are usually treated as separate generalizations.)

- When there are two vowels together, the first usually represents its long sound, and the second is not sounded. (This generalization applies most frequently to *ee, oa, ea, ai: fēed, bōat, bēat, māil.*)
- In words with two vowels, one of which is final *e,* the *e* is usually not sounded and the first vowel is usually long (*tāke, tūbe*).
- *Ay* at the end of a word has the long sound of *ā (may, pay, play).*
- When the only vowel in a word (or accented syllable) comes at the end of the word (or syllable), it usually has its long sound.
- When *y* concludes a word of two or more syllables, it has the long sound of *ē* heard in *lucky, badly.*
  Y functions as a vowel when it:
    Concludes a word that has no other vowel
    Concludes words of more than one syllable (*happy*)
    Follows another vowel (*may*)
- Diphthongs are two adjacent vowels, each of which contributes to the sound heard (h*ou*se, pl*ow*, *oi*l, b*oy*).
- The combination *ow* is sometimes pronounced as long *ō* (sn*ow*, sh*ow*); context provides the major clue to pronunciation.

7

Structural Analysis Skills

Learning to read is a long-term, developmental process, and teaching a total word-analysis skills program is also developmental in nature. Previous chapters have presented data on letter-sound relationships; this chapter continues to deal with letter-sound relationships, but we will also stress other important word-analysis skills that fit under the broad heading of structural analysis. To maintain normal growth in reading, a child must learn to recognize and react to certain features of the written language, including: (a) inflectional endings—*s, ed, ing, ly,* etc.; (b) compound words; (c) plural forms; (d) prefixes—suffixes; (e) syllabication; (f) contractions; and (g) accent within words.

As we have noted, when a child meets a printed word that he does not instantly recognize, he has several options: (a) to sound out the word; (b) to use context clues; (c) to combine these two approaches.

Early in beginning reading, the child adds another option, that of recognizing a root word imbedded among affixes. English orthography utilizes a number of structural changes that occur again and again in thousands of words. In learning to read one must develop expertise in recognizing prefixes, suffixes, and inflectional endings.

To successfully master the structural variations that occur in English orthography, the child must come to the reading task with certain skills and abilities. In essence, he must apply or transfer something he already knows about letter-sounds and word forms to new situations. For example, assume the child can recognize the word *ask,* but has not yet met *asks, asked, asking.* His prior experience and his ability to respond to *ask* should help him in decoding the inflected forms.

While he still has the options of sounding out these new words, he can also use the established response to the word *ask.* If one is reading for meaning, this root-clue plus the contextual demands of the passage will unlock the inflected forms that are used constantly in the child's oral language.

Different readers, however, will require a differing number of experiences and varied amounts of instruction to acquire the necessary insights. For some children, a prefix and suffix added to a known word tends to obscure what is known. In such cases more trials are needed for transfer to take place. All children must have a certain amount of practice in recognizing the visual patterns of words that result from the addition of affixes.

One factor that aids both the learner and the teacher is that a great majority of affixes represent the same sound(s) in thousands of different words. Thus, the major objective in working with structural changes in words is to teach the child to instantly recognize these visual patterns in written English.

Inflectional Endings

The word endings *s* and *ed* represent variations in letter-sound relationships that probably have little impact on learning to read. The fact that final *s* represents the sound of *s* in *asks* and *z* in *dogs* is not a cause of confusion to beginners. Nor is the fact that *ed* in *added, asked,* and *played* is pronounced as *ed, t,* and *d* respectively. The rules that govern these differences are complicated and are much more important to linguists than to native speakers of English whose objective is to learn to read English. Children have never heard, said, or read "The man work-ed hard," or "Where are my glove-s?"

Nonetheless, children will likely need some practice in visual recognition of inflected word forms because of the structural differences between these and known root words.

Adding *s, ed,* and *ing* to Words

1. In the spaces provided, write the word on the left adding *s, ed,* and *ing.*
2. Pronounce each word.

Word	*s*	*ed*	*ing*
walk			
show			
look			
ask			
call			
answer			

load

paint

Adding *er, est,* and *ly* to Words

1. Make new words by adding the endings *er, est,* and *ly* to the root word on the left.
2. Pronounce each word.
3. How do these endings change the meaning of words?

Word	*er*	*est*	*ly*
slow			
light			
warm			
soft			
bright			
calm			

Words Ending with *e*

Drop final *e* before adding a suffix beginning with a vowel.

	+ *ed*	+ *ing*	+ *er*	+ *est*	+ *ous*
bake	baked	baking	baker		
trade	traded	trading	trader		
pale	paled		paler	palest	
fame	famed				famous
late			later	latest	

Adding Suffixes Following *y*

Change *y* to *i* before adding a suffix beginning with a vowel.

Word	*Common endings beginning with a vowel:*			
	-ed	*-er*	*-est*	*-ous*
busy	busied	busier	busiest	
fury				furious
dry	dried	drier	driest	
muddy	muddied	muddier	muddiest	
happy		happier	happiest	
glory				glorious
carry	carried	carrier		

Exception: If the suffix begins with *i*, leave the *y: crying, drying, frying, flying, copy-ing, carrying.*

Doubling Final Consonants

Explain the generalization, "Words that contain one vowel and end with a single consonant (beg, stop, fan) usually double that consonant before adding an ending beginning with a vowel." (As in begged, begging, beggar, stopped, stopping, stopper.)

Exercise: Doubling Consonants

Prepare practice materials such as the following:

Teacher: "Look carefully at the words on lines 1, 2, and 3. Add the same endings to the other words."

	-ed	-ing	-er
1. log	logged	logging	logger
2. dim	dimmed	dimming	dimmer
3. stop	stopped	stopping	stopper
4. pop	_____	_____	_____
5. skip	_____	_____	_____
6. trot	_____	_____	_____
7. bat	_____	_____	_____
8. trap	_____	_____	_____
9. plan	_____	_____	_____
10. spot	_____	_____	_____

Using Context

Teacher: "Each sentence below has a blank space. Complete each sentence using one word in the clue box that will make the sentence correct."

Clue Box for sentences 1–5
walks   walked   walk   walking

1. Can the baby _____?
2. Yes, the baby is _____ now.
3. She _____ yesterday.
4. She _____ every day.
5. She will _____ tomorrow.

Clue Box for sentences 6–10
slow   slowly   slows   slower   slowest

6. Who is the _____ runner on the team?
7. John is very _____ .
8. He is _____ than Tom and Rob.
9. After he runs a while he _____ down.
10. But John is _____ improving.

Teacher: "In the following sentences, write the form of the word that makes the sentence correct."

fast   1. John is _____ than Bill, but Ted is the _____ runner on the team.
kind   2. The mayor is a _____ old gentleman.
cold   3. November is _____ than July.
short   4. If they took the _____ trail they should arrive _____ .
long   5. What is the _____ word in the dictionary?

Teacher: "Each of these sentences is followed by three words. Two of these words will fit in the blank spaces. Read each sentence and fill in the blanks."

Example:

    June is _____ but July is _____ .
    June is __warm__ but July is __warmer__ .

warm
warmer
warmest

    1. John _____ , "Did anyone _____ for me?"

ask
asking
asked

    2. She _____ yesterday and is also _____ today.

paints
painted
painting

    3. Speaking _____ , John said, "Cotton is _____ than linen."

softer
softly
softest

    4. The car _____ at the _____ sign.

stop
stopping
stopped

    5. It _____ yesterday and is _____ now.

rain
rained
raining

Teacher: "In each sentence there is a blank space with a root word below it. Add the proper ending to this word so that it will be correct in the sentence."

Example:
Mother is <u>bringing</u> cookies.

    1. The bird _____ its wings.
               (flap)
    2. We are _____ to leave tomorrow.
               (plan)
    3. We saw a _____ in the woods.
               (hunt)

4. A man who cuts down trees in a forest is called a _____.
   (log)

5. One who traps animals is called a _____ .
   (trap)

6. The little dog was _____ .
   (bark)

7. Who is the best _____ on the baseball team?
   (hit)

8. John is the _____ _____ on the team.
   (fast)   (run)

9. Two boys were _____ in the sand.
   (dig)

10. The _____ it rained the _____ we got.
    (hard)   (wet)

Compound Words

Mastery of compound words is a developmental process. The child meets a few compounds in grade one and an increasing number thereafter. She needs to know that some words are formed by combining two or more words. In most instances she will be familiar with one or both words that make up a compound.

Recognition of compound words is achieved through every type of word-analysis skill (structural analysis, phonic analysis, and context examination). When teaching compound words, each of these aids should be employed. Learning sight words and structural-phonic analysis actually go hand in hand. Keep these points in mind:

- Compound words are part of the child's speaking and meaning vocabulary. When she meets compounds in reading, she will combine recognition and sounding techniques.
- The meaning of many compound words is derived from combining two words.
- The pronunciation of the compound word remains the same as the two combining forms (except for accent or stress).
- Procedures for teaching compound words vary with the instructional level.

Exercises: Building Compound Words

1. Oral Exercise
   Purpose: To provide practice in using compound words.
   Directions: Explain the concept of compound words, that is, combining two words to make a different word.

   Demonstrate on the chalkboard: some + thing = something
                                    some + one = someone
                                    some + time = sometime
   (schoolhouse, barnyard, football, birdhouse, firefighter, etc.)

Teacher: "I'll say a word and you add a word to it to make another word."

1. base _____ (ball)
2. sail _____ (boat)
3. door _____ (way, man, mat)
4. motor _____ (cycle, boat)
5. road _____ (way, side, sign)
6. over _____ (head, board, shoe)
7. moon _____ (light, beam, glow)
8. air _____ (plane, port)
9. bath _____ (tub, house, room)
10. tooth _____ (brush, ache, paste)

2. Seeing Compound Words as Wholes and Breaking Them into Parts
   Teacher: "Each of the words on the left is a compound word. Write the two words found in each compound word."

   Example:

snowman	snow	man
1. waterfall	_____	_____
2. bluebird	_____	_____
3. policeman	_____	_____
4. notebook	_____	_____
5. himself	_____	_____
6. homework	_____	_____
7. anyone	_____	_____
8. seaside	_____	_____
9. turnpike	_____	_____
10. airplane	_____	_____

3. More Compound Words
   Teacher: "Combine one word from the box with a word below the box to form a compound word."

Clue Box			
type	tooth	snap	after
any	grand	bed	light

   _____ ache   _____ one

   _____ noon   _____ writer

   _____ father   _____ shot

   _____ house   _____ room

To provide practice in recognizing and writing compound words, illustrate how the same word can be used in a number of compound words.

Teacher: "Using the word in the first column, write three compound words."

Example:

air	plane	craft	port
	airplane	*aircraft*	*airport*

1. book   case   keeper   worm

   _____   _____   _____

2. door   way   man   mat

   _____   _____   _____

3. candle   light   maker   stick

   _____   _____   _____

4. moon   glow   beam   light

   _____   _____   _____

5. down   town   wind   stream

   _____   _____   _____

6. shoe   lace   horn   maker

   _____   _____   _____

Teacher: "Each line contains one compound word. Underline the compound word and write it on the blank space at the end of the line."

1. children   dancing   hotdog   _____
2. someone   beaches   crawling   _____
3. alike   mousetrap   puzzle   _____
4. downpour   happily   permitted   _____
5. autumn   mistake   handbag   _____

4. Identifying Compound Words
Directions: Some of the following are compound words, and some are two words written together that do not make a word. Have the children underline the compound words.

beehive	ballback	ballpark
anyelse	everyone	everysome
roommate	roompost	signpost
aftermuch	afternoon	afterman
fireplace	photodog	overland
overleft	houseboat	housemake
nearby	overstill	lifeboat

5. Using Context
Directions: Have the children underline each compound word. Then have them draw a line between the two words in each compound (*mail*/*box*).

1. Everyone went to the football game that afternoon.
2. John is upstairs writing in his scrapbook with his ballpoint pen.
3. We ran halfway to the clubhouse without stopping.
4. Frank received a flashlight, a raincoat, and a sailboat for his birthday.

5. He read the newspaper headline, "Big fire at sawmill."
6. They saw the shipwreck from a hilltop near the lighthouse.

6. Directions: Develop a series of sentences in which a common compound will complete the sentence, then have the child read the sentence and write the compound word.

Presentation: Material can be presented orally, or by means of the chalkboard, transparencies, or duplicated exercises. The first exercise is made easy by presenting the compound words in scrambled order above the sentences. In the second exercise, the child provides the words.

baseball	mailbox	bedroom
raincoat	football	seashore

1. Letters are mailed in a _____.
2. The room we sleep in is called a _____.
3. A bat is used in the game of _____.
4. The girls gathered shells at the _____.
5. A _____ field has goalposts at each end of the field.
6. Mother said, "It's raining; be sure and wear your _____."

1. A player can hit a home run in the game of _____.
2. The teacher wrote on the _____ with a piece of chalk.
3. The airplane landed at the _____.
4. The front window in a car is called the _____.
5. The mailman puts mail in our _____.

7. Directions: Have the children add the correct word in sentences 1 and 2, then combine these two words in sentence 3.

Example:

1. The opposite of work is _____. (play)
1
2. In the spring we plant seeds in the _____. (ground)
2
3. We go to the _____ at recess. (playground)
1 & 2

1. Let's take our sleds and play in the _____.
1
2. The pitcher threw the _____ over the plate.
2
3. We like to have _____ fights in the winter.
1 & 2

1. The house we live in is called our _____.
1
2. The opposite of play is _____.
2
3. School work we do at home is called _____.
1 & 2

1. A mailman delivers the _____ .
                                       1
2. He carries the mail in a _____ .
                                        2
3. The mailman carries the mail in a _____ .
                                              1 & 2

Teacher: "Each sentence contains a blank space. Select a word from the clue box that will complete a compound word."

Examples:
Clues: A. grand
         B. snap
         C. house

A. Mother read the letter from _____ father.

B. The letter contained a _____ shot.

C. It showed grandfather in front of a light _____ .

Clue Box			
way	point	wreck	some
brush	house	teller	star

1. John lost his ball _____ pen.

2. The captain gave details about the ship _____ .

3. The sign read, "Don't block the door _____ ."

4. Some of the golfers ate dinner at the club _____ .

5. Susan found a _____ fish on the beach.

6. Grandfather was a great story _____ .

7. _____ one will have to help the guide.

8. Clean the paint _____ when you finish painting.

Working with Plurals

Forming plurals by adding *s, es, (y)ies* results in structural changes in word forms that can be puzzling to children in their early reading experience. Exercises can help children instantly recognize the plurals of common root words.

Adding *s* to Form Plurals

Procedure:

1. Illustrate the singular-plural concept at the chalkboard using any words that add the letter *s* to form a plural (book–book*s*; hat–hat*s*; chair–chair*s*; etc.). Teach the concept, "plural means more than one."

2. Write the plural of the word on the blank space.

cup	_____	game	_____
rat	_____	bag	_____
fan	_____	kitten	_____
boat	_____	comb	_____
desk	_____	nail	_____
rabbit	_____	table	_____
king	_____	ship	_____
crop	_____	sled	_____

3. Prepare materials similar to the illustrations.
4. Read the sentences with the children.

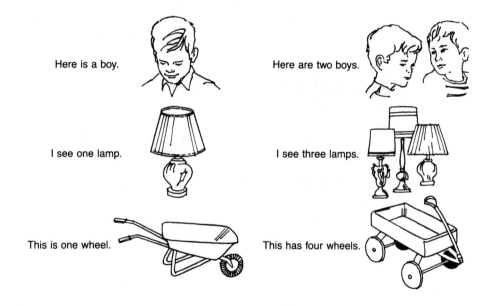

Here is a boy.   Here are two boys.

I see one lamp.   I see three lamps.

This is one wheel.   This has four wheels.

Plurals Formed by Adding *es*

Teach the concept that words ending with *s, ss, ch, sh,* and *x* form plurals by adding *es*. Use the chalkboard or duplicated materials to present material similar to the following.

When do we add *es* to show more than one?
When words end with

ss	*ch*	*sh*	*x*
dress	church	dish	box
dresses	*churches*	*dishes*	*boxes*

Exercise: Forming Plurals

Teacher: "Write the plural for each word."

glass	_____	brush	_____
pass	_____	wish	_____
cross	_____	crash	_____
witch	_____	fox	_____
watch	_____	six	_____
inch	_____	tax	_____

Teacher: "Practice reading these words."

matches	sketches	speeches	benches	waxes
splashes	wishes	batches	ashes	fusses
beaches	kisses	gulches	hisses	birches
bosses	dashes	misses	lashes	gashes

Words Ending with *y*

When a word ends with *y*, its plural is formed by changing the *y* to *i* and adding *es*.

city-cit*ies*   lady-lad*ies*   fairy-fair*ies*

Exercise: Plurals of Words Ending in *y*

Teacher: "Write the plural for each of these words."

baby	_____	party	_____	cherry	_____
puppy	_____	body	_____	buddy	_____
army	_____	fly	_____	berry	_____

Drill on Recognition of Plurals

Teacher: "Each of the following words means 'more than one.' These plurals were formed by adding *s, es,* or (*y*) = *ies*. Read these words as quickly as possible."

porches	foxes	cubs	lunches	watches	witches
girls	benches	guesses	coaches	inches	taxes
speeches	peaches	dresses	answers	matches	candies
funnies	factories	cookies	berries	pennies	armies
buses	glasses	frogs	boxes	brushes	dishes

Other Plural Forms

Some plurals involve vowel changes within the word: *foot-feet; man-men; goose-geese; mouse-mice; tooth-teeth; woman-women.*

For words ending with *f*, change *f* to *v* and add *es: wolf-wolves, shelf-shelves; calf-calves; loaf-loaves; thief-thieves; leaf-leaves.*

Some singular and plural forms are the same spelling: *deer-deer; sheep-sheep; moose-moose.*

For words ending with *o* following a consonant, add *es: potato-potatoes; echo-echoes; hero-heroes; zero-zeroes.*

Exercises: Using Context

Teacher: "The words in column A mean *only one*. If the word under *Clue* means *more than one*, write the plural of the word in column A on the blank space."

Example:

goose	these	geese
A	*Clue*	
lady	one	_____
church	many	_____
city	some	_____
bench	a	_____
bird	a flock of	_____
potato	four	_____
house	this	_____
wolf	a pack of	_____
man	that	_____
sheep	several	_____

Teacher: "In each blank space, write the *plural* form of the underlined word in the sentence."

Examples:
 The <u>woman</u> had been speaking to the _____. (women)
 There were many new _____ in the <u>dress</u> shop. (dresses)

1. The board was a <u>foot</u> wide and ten _____ long.
2. Put this <u>dish</u> in with the clean _____.
3. Many _____ claim to be the "most beautiful <u>city</u>."
4. The young <u>wolf</u> watched the older _____ hunt.
5. This <u>watch</u> is more expensive than the other _____.
6. The <u>spy</u> story was written by two _____.
7. There were many _____ in the <u>bus</u> station.

8. He asked the <u>boy</u> where the other _____ were playing.
9. That <u>lady</u> is president of the _____ group.
10. Put all of the smaller _____ in the largest <u>box</u>.

Teacher: "In each blank space, write the plural of the italicized word."

1. There was one *pony* in the pasture.
   There were two _____ in the pasture.
2. The police captured a *spy.*
   The police captured three _____.
3. Each *lady* bought a hat.
   All the _____ bought hats.
4. One *fly* flew away.
   Both _____ flew away.
5. John lost one *penny.*
   John lost several _____.

Prefixes and Suffixes

As a child progresses in reading, he will meet many words that contain prefixes and suffixes. Teaching aimed at making the child an independent reader will have to deal with structural analysis, phonic analysis, and syllabication. In addition, the teaching of reading will have to focus on the changes in meaning that result when affixes are added to root words.

Many children develop the attitude that they will be unsuccessful in solving longer polysyllabic words, and they give up easily. Thus, their fears are self-fulfilling. One of the objectives of these exercises is to provide hints that will help the reader unlock such words. Children are led to see that English writing contains many pre-fabricated units (prefixes-suffixes). A number of clues are pointed out, namely that these affixes:

Are spelled the same in thousands of different words and thus have the same visual pattern

Have the same pronunciation in different words

Consistently appear before or after a root word

Are usually syllables

The procedures and materials in Example A focus on having the child see and combine root words with prefixes and suffixes while pronouncing the words formed. Examples B and C stress syllabication.

A. Each line begins with a root word to which three prefixes are added. The child pronounces these words, noting the visual patterns resulting from the prefixes.

Root	+ pre	+ re	+ un
pack	prepack	repack	unpack
wind	prewind	rewind	unwind
paid	prepaid	repaid	unpaid

Root	+ dis	+ mis	+ re
place	displace	misplace	replace
use	disuse	misuse	reuse
count	discount	miscount	recount

B. The first word in each column is a root word; the second has a common prefix; the third, a common word ending.

Root	+ dis	+ ment
appoint	dis/appoint	dis/appoint/ment
agree	dis/agree	dis/agree/ment
place	dis/place	dis/place/ment

Root	+ re	+ able
clean	re/clean	re/clean/able
form	re/form	re/form/able
charge	re/charge	re/charge/able

Root	+ in	+ ness
complete	in/complete	in/complete/ness
direct	in/direct	in/direct/ness
visible	in/visible	in/visible/ness
human	in/human	in/human/ness

C. A root word plus suffix + suffix.

Root	+ less	+ ness
use	useless	uselessness
speech	speechless	speechlessness
sight	sightless	sightlessness

Root	+ ful	+ ness
watch	watchful	watchfulness
truth	truthful	truthfulness
play	playful	playfulness

D. This material stresses the structural (visual) changes resulting from adding affixes. It includes some inflected endings taught previously.
   1. Read a line of words in unison with the class.
   2. Have a volunteer read this line of words.
   3. Have similar exercises available for individual practice.

agree	agrees	disagree	disagreement	agreeable
fill	refill	filled	refilled	refilling
place	placed	replaced	replacement	places
honor	honorable	dishonor	dishonorable	honored
hope	hopeless	hopeful	hopefully	hoping

E. For practice in building new words by writing common endings, form a new word by writing the ending shown above each group of words.

ment				ness			
pay	_____	agree	_____	blind	_____	deaf	_____
state	_____	pave	_____	dry	_____	clever	_____
move	_____	treat	_____	close	_____	kind	_____
enjoy	_____	punish	_____	bold	_____	polite	_____
base	_____	excite	_____	calm	_____	like	_____

ful		less		able	
hope	_____	hope	_____	wash	_____
cheer	_____	cheer	_____	honor	_____
doubt	_____	doubt	_____	comfort	_____
grace	_____	cloud	_____	agree	_____
dread	_____	sleep	_____	change	_____

Exercise: Using Context

Teacher: "Note the underlined word in the clue. Add a prefix and suffix to that word so that the new word fits the clue."

Example:
To not deserve <u>trust</u>.   (un)trust(worthy)

Helpers: | dis   un | :: | ful   able   ment   ness |

1. You can't <u>avoid</u> it   _____avoid_____
2. A failure to <u>agree</u>   _____agree_____
3. Can't <u>depend</u> on him   _____depend_____
4. Not being <u>happy</u> is?   _____happi_____
5. Does not tell the <u>truth</u>   _____truth_____
6. Opposite of or lack of <u>honor</u>   _____honor_____

Teacher: "Note the underlined word in the clue. Add an ending to that word so that the new word fits the clue."

Example:
Some <u>doubt</u> that it will happen.   doubt(ful)

Helpers: | able   ful   less   or   ness |

1. No <u>change</u> over the years   change_____
2. Can <u>depend</u> on him   depend_____
3. Always being <u>idle</u>   idle_____
4. Has little or no <u>use</u>   use_____
5. Results in <u>pain</u>   pain_____

6. Shows <u>grace</u> in dancing   grace_____

7. His job is to <u>act</u>   act_____

To help children achieve mastery of root words plus affixes, use these paragraphs for reading practice. Read one paragraph, then select a volunteer to read. Tell students, "As we read each paragraph, note the meaning of the underlined words."

The Governor said, "I <u>doubt</u> that the bridge will be built. <u>Doubtless</u> many of you would like to see it built. However, it is quite <u>doubtful</u> that funds will be available." Informed observers agree that this is <u>doubtlessly</u> true.

An <u>advertiser</u> spends money on <u>advertising</u> because <u>advertisements</u> help to <u>advertise</u> what he has to sell.

A towel will <u>absorb</u> water. This towel is <u>absorbing</u> water. Now it has <u>absorbed</u> about all it can. It <u>absorbs</u> because it is made of <u>absorbent</u> material.

A mountain climber must <u>care</u> about his safety. If one <u>cares</u>, he will be <u>careful</u>, not <u>careless</u>. <u>Carelessness</u> in the face of danger does not lead to a <u>carefree</u> climb. When plans are thought out <u>carefully</u>, one is not likely to act <u>carelessly</u>.

For writing practice, tell students to write a paragraph using all (or as many as possible) of the words on each line.

beauty, beautiful, beautifully
joy, joyful, joyfully, joyous, joyless, joylessly
help, helpful, helpfulness, helpless, helplessness
war, prewar, postwar, prowar, antiwar, warlike

Syllabication

A syllable is a vowel or a group of letters containing a vowel sound which together form a pronounceable unit. The ability to break words into syllables is an important word-analysis skill that cuts across both phonic and structural analysis. Syllabication is an aid in:

Pronouncing words not instantly recognized as sight words

Arriving at the correct spelling of many words

Breaking words at the end of a line of writing

Two major clues to syllabication are prefixes/suffixes and certain vowel-consonant behavior in written words. Thus, the ability to solve the pronunciations represented by many longer printed words is built on the recognition of both structural and phonetic features.

Much of the material regarding prefixes and suffixes can be used for teaching syllabication, as well as visual recognition of word parts. What follows continues to build recognition of prefixes and suffixes but also stresses how these function as syllables. With practice, syllabication tends to become an automatic process. To illustrate, there will be considerable agreement among adult readers when they pronounce the following nonsense words: dismorative, unmurly, interlate, motoption. The syllabication patterns arrived at would probably be: dis·mor·a·tive, un·mur·ly, in·ter·late, mo·top·tion. In addition, there would probably be relatively high agreement as to which syllable was to receive the primary accent: dis·mor'·a·tive, un·mur'·ly, in'·ter·late, mo·top'·tion .

The reader's pronunciation of these nonsense words probably did not involve calling to mind rules that might apply, yet the responses were undoubtedly conditioned by previous learning and experiences that relate to principles of syllabication. Despite numerous exceptions to some generalizations dealing with syllabication, other generalizations may be useful to pupils aspiring to become independent readers.

Generalizations Relating to Syllabication

1. There are as many syllables as there are vowel sounds. Syllables are determined by the vowel sounds heard—not by the number of vowels seen.

	Vowels seen		Vowels heard		Vowels seen		Vowels heard
measure	(4)	mezh'er	(2)	moment	(2)	mō' ment	(2)
phonics	(2)	fon iks	(2)	cheese	(3)	chēz	(1)
write	(2)	rīt	(1)	which	(1)	hwich	(1)
release	(4)	rē lēs	(2)	precaution	(5)	prē kô shun	(3)
skill	(1)	skill	(1)	receive	(4)	rē sēv'	(2)

2. Syllables divide between double consonants—or between two consonants.

hap·pen	can·non	sud·den	ves·sel	vol·ley	com·mand
bas·ket	tar·get	cin·der	har·bor	tim·ber	wig·wam
don·key	pic·nic	gar·den	lad·der	let·ter	sup·per

3. A single consonant between vowels usually goes with the second vowel.

fa mous	ho tel	di rect	ti ger	ce ment	pu pil
ea ger	wa ter	po lice	lo cate	va cant	spi der
be gin	fi nal	be fore	pi lot	li bel	sto ry
pa rade	e lect	re ceive	lo cal	sta tion	be hind

(The previous two generalizations are often combined: Divide between two consonants and in front of one.)

4. As a general rule, do not divide consonant digraphs (*ch*, *th*, etc.) and consonant blends.

teach er	wea*th* er	ma *chine*	se *cret*	a *gree*
bro*th* er	preach er	a*th* lete	coun *try*	cel e *brate*

5. The word endings *-ble, -cle, -dle, -gle, -kle, -ple, -tle, -zle* form the final syllable.

mar ble	mus cle	han dle	sin gle	an kle	tem ple
ket tle	puz zle	no ble	pur ple	bat tle	bu gle

The following list of words can be used in building board or seatwork exercises. Instruct your students to practice these words so they can recognize and pronounce each one instantly. Point out how easy it is to learn to spell the words.

no ble	rat tle	sin gle	han dle	tem ple	an kle
mar ble	ket tle	wig gle	mid dle	ma ple	spar kle
sta ble	ti tle	jun gle	pad dle	ap ple	wrin kle
tum ble	bat tle	strug gle	bun dle	sam ple	sprin kle
trou ble	bot tle	gig gle	fid dle	pur ple	crin kle
fa ble	gen tle	bu gle	bri dle	stee ple	tin kle
dou ble	cat tle	ea gle	nee dle	sim ple	puz zle
rum ble	man tle	an gle	sad dle	un cle	fiz zle
peb ble	set tle	shin gle	kin dle	cir cle	muz zle
bub ble	lit tle	strag gle	pud dle	ve hi cle	daz zle

6. Usually, prefixes and a number of suffixes form separate syllables.

re load ing	un fair	dis agree ment	pre heat ed
hope less	trans port ing	un like ly	ex cite ment

Affixes as Syllables

As we have noted, many prefixes and word endings constitute syllables that are highly consistent in regard to spelling and pronunciation. When children encounter difficulty in attacking and solving longer words, experiences should be provided that help them see the spelling and syllable patterns. The following lessons can help children recognize polysyllabic words that contain a prefix, suffix, or both.

Seeing Syllables in Longer Words

A. Read down each column.

lo	con	dis
lo co	con ver	dis a
lo co mo	con ver sa	dis a gree
lo co mo tive	con ver sa tion	dis a gree ment

B.

lo	con	dis
lo co	con ver	dis a
lo co mo	con ver sa	dis a gree
lo co mo tive	con ver sa tion	dis a gree ment
lo co mo	con ver sa	dis a gree
lo co	con ver	dis a
lo	con	dis
locomotive	*conversation*	*disagreement*

C. Read across each line as quickly as you can.

locomotive	lo	lo co	lo co mo	locomotive
conversation	con	con ver	con ver sa	conversation
disagreement	dis	dis a	dis a gree	disagreement

D. Note the italicized parts of the first word in each column. The words in each column begin and end with the same prefix and suffix, which in every case are pronounced exactly the same. Reading down the columns, pronounce these words as quickly as you can. This practice will help you recognize and sound out words when you meet them in your reading.

con*duction*	*re*fill*able*	*dis*appoint*ment*
conformation	remarkable	disagreement
condensation	reclaimable	disarmament
conservation	recoverable	disarrangement
concentration	redeemable	displacement
conscription	recallable	disfigurement
contraction	respectable	discouragement
contribution	reliable	disenchantment
conviction	renewable	disownment
consolidation	restrainable	discontentment

The following words contain prefixes and suffixes, but the words are in mixed order. Also, some prefixes and suffixes omitted from Part D are introduced. Practice pronouncing the words as quickly as you can.

dishonorable	resentment	discernment	remorseless
relentless	preoccupation	resistant	presumably
premeditate	consolidation	distractible	configuration
reconstruction	distributive	preparatory	reelection
protective	recollection	consignment	disqualification
confederation	presumably	prohibitive	constructive
unseasonable	imperfection	automotive	protectorate
implication	discoloration	concealment	unwholesome

E. Each line consists of long words that contain the same prefix and word ending. The affixes are italicized and the words are broken into syllables. Read each line as quickly as you can, blending the syllables into the proper pronunciation of the word.

con ven *tion,*   *con* sti tu *tion,*   *con* ver sa *tion,*   *con* tri bu *tion*

ex am i na *tion,*   *ex* pe di *tion,*   *ex* cep *tion,*   *ex* hi bi *tion*

dis ap point *ment,*   *dis* a gree *ment,*   *dis* arm a *ment,*   *dis* cour age *ment*

re fill *a ble,*   *re* place *a ble,*   *re* new *a ble,*   *re* pay *a ble*

in ex act *ly,*   *in* sane *ly,*   *in* dis tinct *ly,*   *in* stant *ly*

Abbreviations

Abbreviations represent a special instance of structural (visual) changes that are found in printed material. Children need to understand these concepts about abbreviations:

1. They are a "short form" of writing that represents a longer word or phrase.
2. They are frequently followed by a period.
3. They are not pronounced, but the word the abbreviation stands for is pronounced.

We see	We say	We see	We say
Mr.	Mister	Pres.	President
Dr.	Doctor	Gov.	Governor
Ave.	Avenue	St.	Street

One approach for helping children learn and deal with abbreviations is to present a series of related terms, such as measures, language terms, state names, days of the week or names of the month, titles, etc. (Columns A and B illustrate a series, C presents mixed terms.)

A		B		C	
Sunday	Sun.	inch	in.	abbreviated	abbr.
Monday	Mon.	pound	lb.	abbreviation	abbrev.
Tuesday	Tues.	mile	mi.	building	bldg.
Wednesday	Wed.	quart	qt.	plural	pl.
Thursday	Thurs.	square foot	sq. ft.	Northwest	N.W.
Friday	Fri.	yard	yd.	mountain	mt.
Saturday	Sat.	pint	pt.	Boulevard	Blvd.

Exercises: Abbreviations

Directions: Write a number of abbreviations on the chalkboard. Have volunteers give the words the abbreviations represent.

Example:

Pres.	President
Dr.	Doctor
Ave.	_____
sq. yd.	_____
Gov.	_____
etc.	_____
St.	_____
U.S.	_____

Have the children write the abbreviations for the words listed. If they need help, they can choose from the abbreviations in the box.

		Clue Box		
D.C.	Gov.	Atty.	Prof.	Wk.
Dr.	Bldg.	Ave.	Chap.	Mr.

Mister	_____	Doctor	_____
Building	_____	Governor	_____
Professor	_____	Week	_____
District of Columbia	_____	Avenue	_____
Chapter	_____	Attorney	_____

Teacher: "In the blank space under each underlined word, write the abbreviation of that word."

1. Last <u>Monday</u> the <u>President</u> spoke to the <u>Governor</u>.

_____   _____   _____

2. To write the <u>plural</u> of <u>pound</u> add an s.

_____   _____

3. The <u>doctor</u> has an office on Elm <u>Avenue</u>.

_____   _____

4. The words <u>mile</u>, <u>foot</u>, and <u>quart</u> are measures.

_____   _____   _____

5. The <u>professor</u> lives on <u>Mountain</u> <u>Boulevard</u>.

_____   _____   _____

Recognizing Contractions

In oral language, children both use and understand contractions. In reading, they need to learn the visual patterns involved, along with these facts about contractions:

A contraction is a single word that results from combining two or more words.

A contraction omits one or more letters found in the combining words.

A contraction contains an apostrophe where a letter or letters have been omitted.

A contraction carries the same meaning as the long form it represents, but has its own pronunciation.

Thus, children need practice in seeing and saying the contracted forms, so they can eventually master them as sight words. There are three steps in dealing with contractions: (a) seeing words and contractions together; (b) matching words and contractions; and (c) writing contractions.

Exercises: Contractions

1. Seeing words and contractions together

Teacher: "Look at the two words in the first column and see how they form a contraction when combined in the second column."

Words	Contractions	Words	Contractions
I am	I'm	Do not	Don't
You are	You're	Does not	Doesn't
It is	It's	Was not	Wasn't
I have	I've	Would not	Wouldn't
You have	You've	Could not	Couldn't
They have	They've	Should not	Shouldn't

2. Matching words and contractions

Teacher: "Draw a line from two words under A to the contraction under B."

A	B	A	B
does not	don't	let us	wouldn't
I have	doesn't	would not	wasn't
do not	I've	was not	let's
I am	can't	could not	I'd
cannot	I'm	I would	couldn't

3. Writing contractions

Teacher: "Write the contraction for each of the following word pairs."

They are _____   I have   _____

She is   _____   Should not _____

Must not _____   Here is   _____

Will not _____   They have _____

Teacher: "On the blank space following each sentence, write the contraction for the italicized words."

Example:
Bill *cannot* go swimming. <u>can't</u>

1. *We will* be careful with our campfire. _____
2. Sue *did not* brush her teeth after breakfast. _____
3. *Let us* have a sack race. _____
4. They *could not* catch a fish. _____
5. *I have* eaten my lunch already. _____
6. Larry *does not* play in the street. _____
7. *I am* very happy to see you. _____

8. Karen and Jeff *were not* ready to sing. _____

9. This *is not* my house. _____

10. They *do not* seem very friendly. _____

Finding Little Words in Big Words

In the past, considerable confusion has arisen over a particular practice. It was once quite common, in materials prepared for teachers, to suggest that children be taught to look for little words in big words. The theory was that after a child has learned to recognize smaller words, it would be useful to her as a reader if she would see these smaller units when they were part of larger words. This, it was alleged, would help her solve or pronounce the larger words.

This practice, of course, has only limited utility or justification. It is justifiable when dealing with compound words or known root words to which prefixes or suffixes have been added. In general, however, the habit of seeing little words in big words will actually interfere with sounding out words in a great many cases; this is true even in beginning reading.

To illustrate, let us look at some of the more common "little words." In each of the following, if the child sees and pronounces the little word, she cannot arrive at the pronunciation of the word under attack.

at:	bo at	b at h	pl at e	o at	at e	at omic
	r at e	pot at o	co at	at hlete	he at	
as:	bo as t	ple as e	As ia	co as t	as hore	
on:	on e	t on e	d on e	h on ey	st on e	
he:	he at	he lp	c he st	bat he	t he y	w he at
me:	me at	a me n	ca me	sa me	a me nd	

Hundreds of other examples could be added, using the previous list and other little words: *in, an, it, am, if, us, is, to, up, go, no, lid, are, or.* Little words (or their spellings) occur frequently in larger polysyllabic words, but the pronounceable autonomy of the little words in big words is often lost. Therefore, teaching children to look for little words in big words has little justification from the standpoint of phonic or structural analysis.

Accent

Each syllable in polysyllabic words is not spoken with the same force or stress. These variations in stress are called "accent." The syllable that receives the most stress is said to have the primary accent (car' pen ter). Other syllables in a word may have a secondary accent, or syllables may be unaccented (in' vi ta' tion).

Teaching accent is usually reserved for the later stages of word analysis. The majority of words met in beginning reading consist of one or two syllables; longer words are those a child has probably heard or spoken hundreds of times (*yesterday, grandmother, afternoon, tomorrow, telephone*).

Accent is important in using a dictionary when the objective is to determine a word's pronunciation. It is important in reading when a child meets a word he does not know on sight but has heard and whose meaning he knows. For instance, if a child has heard or used the words *celebration* and *appendicitis* but does not recognize the printed symbols, he may distort the pronunciation through improper syllabication: cē le' bra tion, ce leb' ra tion; or improper accent; ap' pen *di* ci tis.

Skills to be taught include:

1. How to read primary and secondary accent marks in the dictionary.
2. The habit of "trying" different soundings if the first attempt does not result in a known word.
3. The use of clues or rules of accent in attempting the pronunciation of words.

These are some of the clues and rules:

In compound words, the primary accent usually falls on (or within) the first word (sail' boat; wolf' hound; fish' er man; door' way).

In two-syllable words containing a double consonant, the accent usually falls on the first syllable (cop' per; mil' lion; pret' ty; val' ley; sud' den).

When *ck* ends a syllable, that syllable is usually accented (chick' en; rock' et; pack' age; nick' el; mack' er el).

Syllables comprised of a consonant plus *le* are usually not accented (*ble, cle, dle, gle, ple, tle*).

Many of the instances covered by the preceding rules might be summarized under one inclusive generalization: In two-syllable root words, the accent usually falls on the first syllable—except when the second syllable contains two vowels (pa rade'; sur prise'; sus tain'; ma chine'; sup pose').

Prefixes and suffixes are usually not accented (lone' ly; un hap' pi ly; re fresh' ment; dis re spect' ful; re tract' a ble).

Two-syllable words ending with *y* are usually accented on the first syllable (cit' y; ear' ly; ba' by; can' dy; sto' ry; par' ty; fun' ny; mer' ry; tru' ly).

Shift in Accent

Adding suffixes to some longer words may cause a shift in the primary accent. The words in the left-hand column have the primary accent on the first or second syllables, but in the right-hand column, the accent has shifted.

u' ni verse	u ni ver' sal
mi' cro scope	mi cro scop' ic
vac' ci nate	vac ci na' tion
ac' ci dent	ac ci den' tal
con firm'	con fir ma' tion

We can thus generalize that in many longer words, the primary accent falls on the syllable before the suffix. (Exception: In most cases the primary accent falls two syllables before the suffix *-ate*: ag' gra vate; dom' i nate; ed' u cate; hes' i tate; med' i tate; op' er ate.)

Homographs and accent shift (Homo = same; graph = to write; thus, homograph = same writing). Homographs are words with identical spellings, different meanings, and, in some cases, different pronunciations. Note in the following sentences that usage or context determines the pronunciation. (Changes may occur in accent or in both accent and syllabication.) For example, present = pre/sent' or pres'/ent; content = con/tent' or con'/tent.

1. The mayor was *present* to *present* the awards.
2. The editor was not *content* with the *content* of the article.
3. Always be careful to *address* the letter to the correct *address*.

These words can be used in exercises when context is provided:

protest—protest	annex—annex
perfect—perfect	rebel—rebel
convict—convict	object—object
permit—permit	contract—contract
excuse—excuse	produce—produce
subject—subject	conduct—conduct

Stress on Words within Sentences

When working on accent of syllables within words, one might point out the parallel of stress on words within sentences. While this is not usually seen as a word-analysis skill, it is a most important factor in mastering the reading process. Concomitant teaching of accent and stress may help the child understand both concepts. Simple sentences might be placed on the board. Children should read the sentences, place added stress on each underlined word, and note the effect of the stress on the melody of the sentence.

<u>This</u> is very bad news.
This is very bad <u>news</u>.
This is <u>very</u> bad news.
This is very <u>bad</u> news.

Use of the Dictionary—As a Word Attack Skill

As children become independent readers, they are likely to meet a number of words that:

They do not know or use in their speaking vocabularies

They cannot easily solve by applying phonic generalizations

Since the dictionary is a source for pronunciation of words, certain dictionary skills are, in effect, word-analysis skills. Effective use of the dictionary involves learning the speech equivalents of visual symbols, including primary and secondary accent marks; diacritical marks, such as the macron (-) (make = māk); the breve (˘) (ăt); and the schwa (ə) (ten dər).

Different dictionaries and glossaries in textbooks may use a variety of symbols, or phonetic spellings, all of which will have to be mastered. For example:

technique: tek nēk; tĕk nēk; tek neek
temperament: tem′ pər ə mənt; tĕm pēr ment

(For a discussion of the schwa sound, see chapter 6).

The same pronunciation key of the dictionaries the children use should be taught. The dictionary will be of little value in arriving at the correct pronunciation of words if these various symbols are not mastered.

Summary

Teaching the decoding process involves more than just letter-sound relationships. Children must also learn to recognize and respond quickly to a number of frequently occurring visual patterns found in English writing. These include inflectional endings, plurals, contractions, abbreviations, prefixes, and suffixes.

After many experiences with affixes (which are also syllables), successful readers develop the ability to treat these word parts as units rather than decoding the same set of letters separately each time they encounter the letters. Thus, in teaching structural analysis skills, the goal is to provide experiences that lead the child to this type of behavior. The structural changes that occur over and over in English writing must be instantly recognized. Fortunately, many of these high frequency affixes have a high degree of consistency in both their visual patterns and sounds.

References

Adams, M. J. (1990). *Beginning to read: Thinking and learning about print.* Cambridge, MA: MIT Press.

Bailey, M. H. (1967). The utility of phonic generalizations in grades one through six. *Reading Teacher, 20,* 413–418.

Bloomfield, L., & Barnhart, C. (1961). *Let's read: A linguistic approach.* Detroit, MI: Wayne State University Press.

Burmeister, L. E. (1968). Vowel pairs. *Reading Teacher, 21,* 445–452.

Burrows, A., & Lourie, Z. When two vowels go walking. *Reading Teacher, 17,* 79–82.

Clymer, T. (1963). The utility of phonic generalizations in the primary grades. *Reading Teacher, 16,* 252–258.

Cunningham, P. M. (1990). The names test: A quick assessment of decoding ability. *Reading Teacher, 44,* 124–129.

Downing, J. A. (1963). *Experiments with Pitman's initial teaching alphabet in British schools.* New York: Initial Teaching Alphabet Publications.

Downing, J. A. (May, 1965). Common misconceptions about i.t.a. *Elementary English, 42.*

Downing, J. A. (December, 1967). Can i.t.a. be improved? *Elementary English, 44,* 849–855.

Emans, R. (1967). The usefulness of phonic generalizations above the primary grades. *Reading Teacher, 20,* 419–425.

Flesch, R. (1955). *Why Johnny can't read.* New York: Harper.

Fries, C. C. (1963). *Linguistics and reading.* New York: Holt, Rinehart, & Winston.

Fries, C. C. (1965). Linguistics and reading problems at the junior high school level. *Reading and Inquiry,* International Reading Association Procedings 10, 244–247.

Gattengo, C. (1962). *Words in color.* Chicago: Learning Materials.

Griffith, P. L., & Olson, M. W. (1992). Phonemic awareness helps beginning readers break the code. *Reading Teacher, 45,* 516–523.

Hayes, R. B., & Nemeth, J. S. (1965). *An attempt to secure additional evidence concerning factors affecting learning to read.* USOE Cooperative Research Project, No. 2697, p. 34.

Heilman, A. W. (1977). *Principles and practices of teaching reading,* 4th ed. Columbus, OH: Merrill/Macmillan.

Mazurkiewicz, A. J. (September, 1964). Lehigh-Bethlehem-I/T/A study interim report six. *Journal of the Reading Specialist, 4,* 3–6.

Newman, J. M., & Chruch, S. M. (1990). Myths of whole language. *Reading Teacher, 44,* 20–26.

Oaks, R. E. (1952). A study of the vowel situations in a primary vocabulary. *Education, 72.*

Pollard, R. (1889). *Pollard's synthetic method.* Chicago: Western Publishing House.

Reading Teacher. (1991). Beginning to read: A critque by literacy professionals and a response by Marilyn Jager Adams. *44,* 366–395.

Samuels, S. J. (1988). Decoding and automaticity: Helping poor readers become automatic at word recognition. *Reading Teacher, 41,* 756–760.

Smith, F. (1973). *Psycholinguistics and reading.* New York: Holt, Rinehart, & Winston.

Stahl, S. A. (1992). Saying the "P" word: Nine guidelines for exemplary phonics instruction. *Reading Teacher, 45,* 618–625.

Stahl, S. A., Osborn, J., & Lehr, F. (1990). *Beginning to read: Thinking and learning about print—a summary.* Champaign, IL: University of Illinois.

Index

Abbreviations, 133–34
Accent
  generalizations related to, 137
  shift in, 137–38
Affixes, working with, 126–29
Alphabetic principle, 2
Auditory discrimination, 43–49
  final sounds in words, 48–49
  initial sounds, 44
  rhymes, working with, 45–48
  Augmented Roman Alphabet, 12

Bailey, Mildred H., 7
Barnhart, Clarence, 18, 20
Blends (clusters), consonant, 63–68
Bloomfield, Leonard, 10, 18
Burmeister, Lou E., 7
Burrows, Alvina, 7

Children learn to read, how, 26–28
Clymer, Theodore, 7, 95
Code cracking
  alternative approaches to, 12–23
  defined, 3
Compound words, 118–22
Consonant letter-sound relationships,
  51–83

blends, teaching, 63–68
consonants not sounded, 80–82
doubling final before vowels, 116–18
end of words, 73–74
initial position, in, 52–63
irregularities, 77–82
Context clues and phonic clues
  exercises for teaching, 59–63
  mental substitution, 55–58
  minimal phonic clues, 58–59
  working together, 59–63
Context, using, 26, 30–31, 59–61, 65–68,
  71–72, 74–76, 88–90, 97–99,
  108–10, 116–18, 128–29
Contractions, 134–36

Dale List of 769 Easy Words, 52
Dictionary, use of, 138–39
Digraphs
  context clues, teaching with, 71–73
  defined, 3
  initial consonant, 68–73
  word endings, 75–77
Diphthongs
  defined, 3
  teaching, 105–6

Dolch Basic Sight Word Test, 52
Downing, John A., 16

Emans, Robert, 7

Flesch, Rudolph, 11, 12
Fries, Charles C., 19
Fun with language, exercises, 61–63,
72–73, 90–91, 99, 101

Grapheme-phoneme relationship, 3

Hancock, Malcolm, 86
Hayes, Robert B., 16
Heilman, Arthur W., 12
Homonyms, 107–10

Inflectional endings, 114–18
Initial Teaching Alphabet (i.t.a.), 12–16
instructional program, 13–16
methodological practices, 14
orthography, 13
postponing the difficult, 14–16
respelling of words, 15
Issues in phonics instruction
necessity of phonic skills, 32
optimum amount of phonics, 33–34
overreliance on phonics, 34
sight word teaching, 34

Language exercises
fun with language, 61–63, 72–73,
90–91, 99, 101
using context, 59–61, 65–68, 71–72,
74–75, 97, 108–10, 116–18,
125–26, 128–29
Let's Read, 18, 20
Letter sound relationships
consonants, 51–83
variability, 5, 77–82, 102–7
vowels, 83–112
Linguistic (regular spelling) approach,
16–21
beginning instruction only, 21
meaning waived, 18
phonics, opposition to, 19
vocabulary control, 17
Little words in big words, 136
Lourie, Zyra, 7

Mazurkiewicz, Albert J., 16
Mental substitution, initial sounds, 55–58
Morpheme, defined, 3

Nemeth, Joseph S., 16

Oaks, Ruth E., 7, 95
Overreliance on one skill, 34

Phoneme, defined, 4
Phonetic method
defined, 4
discussed, 11
sight word method vs., 11
Phonics
history and controversy, 9–23
limitations of, 4–7
purpose of, 1
terminology, 24
Phonics instruction
issues in, 32–34
optimum account of, 33
overreliance on, 34
principles to apply, 35
prerequisites for teaching, 37–49
previous experiences foreign to, 26
sequence, 51–52
Picture clues, 29
Picture dictionary, 54
Pitman, Sir James, 12
Plurals, working with, 122–25
Pollard, Rebecca, 10
Principles of instruction, 35
Programmed reading, 21–22

Reading, essential skills for, 27
Regular spelling concept, defined, 17
Rhyming sounds, 45–48

Schwa, defined, 4
Sight vocabulary, 4
Sight word method, 11–12
Smith, Frank, 33
Structural analysis, 113–39
abbreviations, 133–35
accent, 136–38
affixes, working with, 126–29
compound words, 118–22
contractions, 134–36
defined, 113

Structural analysis, continued
    dictionary use, 138–39
    final consonants, doubled, 116–18
    inflectional endings, 114–18
    plurals, working with, 122–25
    syllabication, 129–32
Syllabication
    clues to, 129
    generalizations related to, 130
    teaching, 129–32
Synthetic Method, 10

Unknown words, responses to, 26
Utility of "rules," 5–6

Variability of letter sounds
    consonants, 77–80
    homonyms, 107–10
    vowels, 5–6, 102–4
Visual discrimination, 37–42
    matching capital and lowercase letters,
      39–40
    matching letter forms, 38–42

word forms, 39, 42
Vowel letter-sounds, 85–112
    diphthongs, 105–6
    exceptions to rules, 102–6
    final *e* generalization, 99–101
    long (glided) sound, 95–101
    minimal contrast, 91–94
    overteaching, 85–86
    schwa sound, 110
    short vowel sounds, 87–94
    single final vowels, 101–2
    "r" controller, 103
    sequence in teaching, 86–87
    visual patterns as cues, 95–97

Why Johnny Can't Read, 11
Word analysis skills
    overview, 28–32
    skills in combination, 30–32
    structural analysis, 29–30
    word configuration clues, 28–29
Word families, 88–89
Words in Color, 22–23